# Young Linguists in Dialogue

The First Conference

# Young Linguists in Dialogue

## The First Conference

Edited by Ewa Willim

Jagiellonian University Press

would be sacrificed for the sake of a perlocution-driven equivalent effect (Nida 1964/2004: 156; Rieu and Philips 1954). Again, emphasis would be on intelligibility of the message and on minimising the audience's processing effort.

The question arises as to whether a message always needs to be made optimally relevant for the audience in the process of being relayed across languages and cultures. In other words, is the secondary sender (Reiss 1971/2004: 168) obliged to tailor the linguistic material with the mini-max programme (cf. Levy 1967/1989) in mind?

That the relevance of verbal stimuli is something to be strived for in intralingual communication is hardly controversial. Objections could be raised, however, as to whether in translation, viz. interlingual mode of communication, the mechanics (e.g. parties' motivation) and hence the determinants of success, are the same.

The problem of balancing processing effort and contextual effects is clearly reflected in the translation strategies employed to render those culturally--motivated ST elements which might make utterances more costly for the target audience to process. The debate about how to deal with 'the foreign' in translation has now continued for at least two centuries.[2] As Schleiermacher's (1813/2004: 49) famous metaphor has it, the choice is primarily between two options: "either the translator leaves the author in peace as much as possible and moves the reader toward him; or he leaves the reader in peace as much as possible and moves the writer toward him."[3]

Since Schleiermacher, many translation theoreticians have tackled the issue, but the discussion on handling the exotic constituents in translation has remained fundamentally twofold as in Nida's (1964, 1964/2004) dynamic and formal equivalence, House's (1977/1981) covert and overt translation, Newmark's (1981) communicative and semantic translation, Nord's (1991) instrumental and documentary translation, Toury's (1995) acceptable and adequate translation, or Venuti's (1995) domestication and foreignisation. With a degree of simplification, all these dyads display a regularity: the translator can either strive for fluency by curtailing the foreignness of the TT or else design a more exacting piece. Viewed through the prism of relevance, the former strategy entails cutting down on the audience's processing effort, thus aiming at optimal relevance.

Consequently, if translation were to be identified with ordinary communication, the first method would have to be advocated; yet, as this paper attempts to point out, this option should not be given unassailable precedence. To quote

[2] Its roots could probably be traced back to Cicero's (46 BC/1960) distinction between the interpreter and the orator.

[3] The translation presented here preserves the nineteenth century assumption that both authors and readers are necessarily male.

This volume was supported by the Jagiellonian University – Institute of English Philology and the Faculty of Philology

REVIEWER
*Dr hab. Elżbieta Chrzanowska-Kluczewska, prof. UJ*



ISBN 978-83-233-2824-7

WYDAWNICTWO UNIWERSYTETU JAGIELLOŃSKIEGO

www.wuj.pl

Wydawnictwo Uniwersytetu Jagiellońskiego
Redakcja: ul. Michałowskiego 9/2, 31-126 Kraków
tel. 12-631-18-81, 12-631-18-82, fax 12-631-18-83
Dystrybucja: ul. Wrocławska 53, 30-011 Kraków
tel. 12-631-01-97, tel./fax 12-631-01-98
tel. kom. 0506-006-674, e-mail: sprzedaz@wuj.pl
Konto: PEKAO SA, nr 80 1240 4722 1111 0000 4856 3325

# CONTENTS

# ACKNOWLEDGEMENTS

Many thanks go to Professor Elżbieta Mańczak-Wohlfeld, who, as Head of the Institute of English Philology at the Jagiellonian University of Kraków, supported the organization of *The First Conference of Young Linguists in Dialogue* both financially and intellectually.

We are also extremely grateful to Professor Elżbieta Tabakowska, whose permission to use the premises of the UNESCO Chair for Translation Studies and Intercultural Communication provided the conference with a venue.

We would also like to express our gratitude to Professor Ewa Willim for her opening lecture entitled *Revisiting Linguistic Determinism: Number in Language and Cognition* and for her work on editing the volume.

The proceedings volume owes a good deal to the anonymous referees, who were generous enough to devote their time and effort to reviewing the papers. Their efforts and advice are greatly appreciated.

Last, but not least, we thank everyone whose enthusiasm and support contributed to the organization of the conference.

*Organizers and Participants*

# PREFACE

The present volume contains selected contributions to the *First Conference of Young Linguists in Dialogue* held at the Jagiellonian University of Kraków in April 2008. The conference was initiated by the Linguistics Section of the Jagiellonian University Students' English Society in close co-operation with the Gavagai Student Society at the Chair of the English Language and Applied Linguistics of the University of Łódź and it is planned to take place annually in different universities across Poland. The aim of the *Young Linguists in Dialogue* series is to bring together students from various departments of English in Poland and present their research in linguistics.

The papers in this volume were chosen as a result of a selection process in which they were reviewed by specialists in the fields to which the topics that they address pertain. Of eleven presentations given at the conference, nine are included in this volume.

The contributions discuss a wide range of issues, embracing formal aspects of the theory of language as well as topics of interest in applied linguistics, in particular in foreign language teaching, translation theory and linguistic stylistics. They proffer advances in two directions: either the papers provide an up-to-date resource on current research on the chosen topic intended for beginners in the specialist area, or they contribute to the understanding of particular problems in the description and theory of language that may be of interest both for beginners and for specialists in the chosen domain of inquiry.

**Paweł Błaszczyk** compares the analysis of a literary text that can be conducted in two different traditions in literary criticism: literary structuralism and cognitive poetics. Focusing on the narrative structure of folk tales, he argues that while both perspectives offer a similar analysis, Peter Stockwell's cognitive schema theory allows for a more flexible account, which is free from the confines of the formulaic construction that underlies Vladimir Propp's plot-analysis.

**Mikołaj Deckert** explores the problem of communicability in linguistically and culturally incompatible contexts. Focusing on the significance of the relevance theory principles of inferential communication for the translator's attempt to achieve communicative resemblance between the original and the translated text, he argues that intentional transmission of information in inter--linguistic and inter-cultural communication is partly at odds with Dan Sperber and Deirdre Wilson's communicative principle of relevance.

**Dobromiła Jagiełła** looks at formal approaches to inter-nominal referential dependencies in the generative paradigm, focusing on Noam Chomsky's classic Binding Theory and its rival, the Binding Theory of Carl Pollard and Ivan Sag. Based on data from Polish, which does not provide clear evidence for logophors, she cautions against exempting long-distance anaphors from grammatical constraints on the distribution and interpretation of referentially dependent nominal expressions.

**Marek Majer** surveys the case-system of Proto-Germanic with a view to establishing whether the locative can be taken to be a distinct morphological and semantic case. On the basis of evidence from Old English, he considers an analysis of the Proto-Germanic case-system with the locative case distinct from the instrumental as a plausible research scenario.

**Marta Ruda** investigates recent advances in psycholinguistics concerned with the influence of processing the grammar of a foreign language (L2) on the processing and production of a bilingual speaker's native language (L1). She presents the results of various experiments devoted to the study of parsing strategies, the influence of priming, and the effects of language attrition in bilinguals and considers the implications that such studies may have for the hypothesis that L2 has an influence on the syntactic processing and production of L1.

**Olga Trendak** readdresses the well-known controversy connected with the nature of grammar instruction in foreign language teaching. Her aim is to present current views on whether the key to success with grammatical competence in a foreign language is deductive or inductive grammar teaching and learning, highlighting both the strong and the weak points of either perspective on grammar instruction discussed in recent SLA studies.

**Radosław Turniak** takes up the problem of intertextuality, highlighting its intersemiotic character. He argues against a narrow approach to text that takes it to be exclusively linguistic in nature and illustrates musical intertexts appearing in poetry mainly from three music genres: blues, jazz and pop music. As knowledge of musical intertexts can enrich the analysis of poetry, it is important for literary critics and translators.

**Jakub Wosik** presents the special features of consecutive interpreting against other types of interpreting, focusing on the form and function of note-taking. The theoretical guidelines for note-taking in consecutive interpreting, mainly due to Jean-François Rozan, are reappraised against the results of a small survey among beginner and experienced consecutive interpreters, which shows that note-taking is a personal strategy for the interpreter to decide on rather than a strict procedure that must be followed.

**Sławomir Zdziebko** presents a down-to-earth introduction to basic concepts and mechanisms of CVCV Phonology, providing the reader with details of a popular phonological model assumed in a wide range of studies, namely Tobias Sheer's Lateral Theory of Phonology. Among the concepts and mechanisms discussed in the paper are syllabic constituent structure, empty nuclei, government and licensing as well as some phonological processes both at the syllable and melody levels. The introduction aims at preparing beginner readers for entry to the current concerns and debates in phonological theory.

*Ewa Willim*
*Editor*

*Paweł Błaszczyk*
Jagiellonian University, Kraków

# STRUCTURAL AND COGNITIVE POETICS: A COMPARISON

## 1. Introduction

Literary analysis that pays greater attention to the text itself than to more or less intuitive ideas about its meaning is a fairly recent invention. Its origin goes back to the famous *Cours de Linguistique Générale* published in 1916, three years after Ferdinand de Saussure's death. The book became an inspiration for specialists in literature convinced that literary studies should be scientific rather than essayistic in nature and who strived to provide literary scholars with tools that would enable them to be more scientific. These theoreticians of literature wanted to analyse texts having at their disposal objective, verifiable methods. Thus, the concept of structure was born, a notion that stems from the belief that literature is a system, because it stems from language, which is also an organized entity. As Sturrock (2003: 99) observes: "literary structuralism is not the novelty which its opponents claim it to be. It is, rather, the latest, unusually sophisticated stage (...) form of literary criticism that has existed since Aristotle." This way of approaching literature, highly sophisticated indeed, had been developing largely unchallenged until the last decade of the 20$^{th}$ century, when a new school was born, namely, cognitive poetics. Although again not quite revolutionary and openly acknowledging its resemblance with structuralist poetics (Gavins and Steen 2003: 5–8), cognitive poetics offers a markedly distinct way of approaching the text based on cognitive linguistics, itself a more recent development in the study of language.

Although the sources of inspirations for the two approaches to literary texts are different, not to say antithetical, it seems that in many respects they arrive at quite similar results, even if obtained within distinct paradigms. In this article, I take a closer look at what exactly the differences between structuralist and cognitive poetics are and try to establish whether we can really say that cognitive linguistics shows any signs of development compared with its predecessor. I will try to compare some selected aspects of the linguistic foundations of the two schools, the way they treat meaning and finally, moving from theory to practice, I will compare the plot-analysis method as presented by Vladimir Propp (1928/1984) in his famous *Morphology of the Folk Tale* with the schema and scenario theory in Peter Stockwell's (2006) rendering.

## 2. Linguistic foundations

As already mentioned, the cornerstone of structuralism is *Cours de Linguistique Générale*, presenting Ferdinand de Saussure's seminal lectures on linguistics. It introduces the now widely known division of language into *langue* and *parole*, defining the former as "a system, an institution, a set of interpersonal rules and norms" and the latter as "the actual manifestation of the system in speech and writing" (Culler 1989: 8). This division, later renamed by Noam Chomsky as *competence* and *performance*, basically corresponds to the idea that there is a coherent, rule-governed whole underlying all actual manifestations of language and consequently, also of literature. As a result, the aim of the literary critic is to look beyond the surface and search for invariants, regularities and general rules. It is assumed that literature (and entire culture) is, to use de Saussure's nomenclature, a *signifiant*, a semiotic device, a form by means of which a given meaning is expressed. It is also important that, from a structuralist standpoint, the form is a purely arbitrary construct as there is usually (onomatopoeic words being a notable exception) no natural relationship between the form of a word and its denotation. For example, what is referred to in English with the word *butterfly*, in Polish is referred to with *motyl* and in Finnish with *perhonen*.

Cognitive linguistics takes a fundamentally different perspective on language. Its main tenet is that all language is context-dependent, where *context* is understood as the entire extra-textual reality. As Stockwell (2006: 2) puts it:

> We think in forms that we do and we say things in the ways that we do, because we are all roughly human-sized containers of air and liquid with our main receptors at the top of our bodies. Our minds are *embodied* not just literally but also figuratively, finally clearing away the mind-body distinction of much philosophy (...).

What is meant by this is the belief that all utterances, from single words to novels, are the expression of the way we perceive and organise our perception of the world in which we live, which in turn cannot be separated from our somatic experience. Thus, while structuralist linguistics looks up to mathematics as a source of inspiration, cognitive linguistics is mostly influenced by psychology. This results in a less formal approach to language, which, according to the opponents of cognitivism, diminishes the scientific value of this paradigm. Nevertheless, cognitivism opens up the possibility to investigate a wider range of phenomena which have hitherto evaded analysis. This may be seen, among other things, in the case of meaning-analysis.

## 3. The problem of meaning in structuralism and cognitive linguistics

To illustrate the structuralist approach to meaning, let us take a closer look at the theory proposed by Algirdas J. Greimas (Culler 1989: 75–96). Striving to provide a tool for semantic analysis, Greimas posited that every lexeme has an invariant core, which is established by extracting the common features, or "the essence" of the word present in all its possible readings in a given corpus. All changes in meaning result from attaching to this core contextually-conditioned features called *semes*. Roughly speaking, a *seme* is an attribute chosen from two opposite features such as [male] vs. [female], or [good] vs. [bad]. The semantic analysis consists of two steps, namely, identifying the core and deciding what kind of attribute is used in a given context of use. For example, consider the following pair of sentences:

(1) The dog barked at me.
(2) The man barked at me.

The core meaning of *to bark* can be determined as 'a sharp, vocal noise' and the *semes* in question as consisting of the attributes [animal] and [human], respectively. This might seem a very neat tool for semantic analysis, but as Culler (1989) points out, it has two major disadvantages. Firstly, the analysis requires compiling a list of all possible attributes and arranging them in a 'semetic' way and, secondly, it simply does not work, even in the case of the lexical items provided by Greimas. In his critique of Greimas's theory, Culler (1989: 78) provides the following example from French:

(3) La police aboie après le criminal.
the police barks after the criminal
'The police chase the criminal.'

(3) does not mean that the police bark after (*aboie après*) a criminal, but that they "chase him with the tenacity of hounds that have taken the scent and are in full cry" (Culler 1989: 78). It becomes a really arduous task to formulate in a formal fashion the link between 'barking', 'speaking loudly' and 'pursuing'.

In fact, "the meaning is [...] constituted in deviation from the listed lexical features" and "semantics [should] be able to account for the deviations and transitions" (Fokkema and Kunne-Ibsch 1979: 73).

Cognitive linguistics seems capable of explaining such changes in a more regular fashion, thanks to the radial model of meaning (Tabakowska 1995: 46–56). This model is based on the idea that metaphor is a basic cognitive tool, allowing people to organise and classify new experience. Thus, the lexical item *key* understood both as 'the key that opens the front door' and as 'the key to the exercises' need not be treated as two separate lexemes, but as two senses of a single lexeme which are related by metaphorical extension. Similarly, the above-mentioned examples of 'barking' can be analysed either as involving a simple metaphorical extension, or, alternatively, as resulting from a metonymical extension: as the activity of barking is very often connected with the activity of chasing, the mental proximity may be the vehicle of extension of meaning. And although this method rules out the possibility of formulaic description, it shows that different meanings of a word are not accidental, but can be traced down by means of cognitive tools.

### 3.1. Comparing the approaches: the analysis of myths

Having briefly examined the theoretical background of the two schools of thought, let us now have a look at how theory influences practical analysis. As mentioned in section 1, the objects of comparison are Propp's (1928/1984) structural approach to the analysis of the myth, and the schema and scenario theory proposed by Stockwell (2006). This choice is motivated by the fact that both theories have received extensive coverage and, more importantly, because they seem to display a considerable level of convergence.

In his approach to the structure of folk tales, Propp (1928/1984) claimed that every folk tale is composed of the so-called *functions* (cf. also Fokkema and Kunne-Ibsch 1979: 61–64). According to him, a function is "an act of a character, defined from the point of view of its significance for the course of action." Such functions "serve as stable, constant elements in a tale, independent of how and by whom they are fulfilled" and as such "constitute the fundamental components of a tale"(Propp 1928/1984: 21). For example, the sentences in (4) and (5) can be represented on a more abstract level of analysis as shown in (6):

(4) The old man gives Sučenko a horse; the horse carries Sučenko to another kingdom.

(5) A king gives an eagle to a hero; the eagle carries the hero away to another kingdom.

(6) Someone [1] gives a hero [2] a magical agent [3], which carries him away.

In (6), [1], [2] and [3] can be filled with different elements (or, to usePropp's nomenclature: dramatis personae) which do not change the whole structure of a folk tale. However, according to Propp, the number of such functions is limited to thirty one altogether. Crucially, their sequence in a fairy tale is fixed. The main disadvantage of this approach is that by claiming that this function-division is applicable only to folk tales and not to literature in general, Propp drastically narrows the area to which the method could be applied. In addition, this analysis does not seem to include all the elements important for the creation of a given situation. Propp mentions only dramatis personae, or the actors, and pays little attention to defining the role of the context and/or objects involved. Only dramatis personae find their way to the description of the narrative event. Furthermore, the approach leads to certain problems with classification. According to Propp (1928/1984: 22), "tales with identical functions can be considered as belonging to one type." At the same time, he mentions that there is practically no variation as to the sequence of functions in a tale. While this may be true with regard to the folk tale, the question arises whether it could be applied to other types of writing without running the risk of multiplying the literary divisions ad infinitum.

Cognitive poetics, in turn, provides literary scholars with a tool of greater flexibility, namely, schemata. Not only do these tools maintain what is valuable in Propp's theory, but at the same time they open new possibilities. In cognitive linguistics, a *schema* is "a schematised representation of detailed experiences" (Stockwell 2006: 8). What this means is that every successful or unsuccessful operation in our life is classified and organized so that the next time we encounter a similar situation, we can act without undue hesitation. Stockwell (2006: 10–11) explains the reasons for the success of the schema theory to preserve what is valuable in Propp's analysis in the following way:

> The framework includes a set of categories to operationalise the details of a schema. There are various kinds of 'slots' that are associated with any particular script and are assumed to be in operation when the schema is going. These are 'props', 'participants', 'entry conditions', 'results' and the 'sequence of events.'

As we can clearly see, there is a striking similarity between the two theories. In both of them we have certain 'slots' which can be filled with different attributes. Where, then, does the advantage of the schema theory over that of Propp's lie? The answer to this question lies in the dynamic character of schemata, which is necessitated by the fact that in our life we usually encounter many similar, yet distinct situations. If schemata were deprived of their dynamic nature, there would be no sense in having them, because each new element would lead to creating a completely new schema and obviously the human brain aims at simplicity and economy.[1]

According to cognitive scholars, to protect itself from such inefficiency, the human brain has come up with the option of *schema refreshment*. This feature allows schemas to modify their internal structure rather than construct themselves anew when faced with a new element. With such a reservation made, schemata at first glance seem to be an ideal tool for literary analysis. However, this is not so obvious, because as Stockwell (2006:11) rightly remarks, "the schema theory is based on commonality, whereas high quality literature tends to be based on uniqueness." Schema refreshment fills the rift between the two tendencies, showing that it is precisely thanks to schemata that we can accommodate new experience, not only in real life, but also within the narrative.

This point can be illustrated with the stages of reception of *The Trial* by Franz Kafka. From the very first words the reader's interest is piqued by the fact that K, the main hero, has been accused without an obvious reason. This is a very clear example of a schema, the schema of LEGAL PROCEDURE. Our experience tells us that in order for somebody to be accused there must exist an entry condition of the law being broken by the person in question. It turns out that one of the reasons why the reader pursues the narrative with increasing interest is the desire to understand the destabilisation of the above-mentioned schema. But the narrative itself is insufficient for refreshing the schema. In order to resolve the cognitive impasse, the reader must resort to his or her knowledge of the surrounding world and try to cope with literary nonsense. It is this flexibility and multi-dimensionality of our literary competence that enables the reader to refresh the schema as well as to create a new one.

## 4. Conclusion

In this paper, I have demonstrated that structuralist and cognitive poetics seem to have a lot in common despite having completely divergent linguistic foundations. The reason for the similarities seems to be that in striving to free literary analysis from wishy-washy essayism, both perspectives employ formal linguistics tools, thus taking a scientific approach to the study of literature.

[1] For example, there would be no one 'restaurant schema,' but rather a whole set of them, including schemas for restaurants with spoons, restaurants without spoons, restaurants with and without tables, etc.

However, this does not mean that cognitive poetics should be viewed merely as a structuralism relabelled. The fact that cognitive linguistics is cognitive has profound implications, because it allows for a more flexible, yet very regular and coherent description of phenomena which have hitherto remained outside the scope of traditional approaches.

## References

Culler, J. (1989). *Structuralist Poetics*. London: Routledge.

Fokkema, D. W., Kunne-Ibsch, E. (1979). *Theories of Literature in the Twentieth Century.* London: Hurst & Company.

Gavins, J., Steen, G. (eds.) (2003). *Cognitive Poetics in Practice*. London: Routledge.

Propp, V. (1928/1984). *Morphology of the Folk Tale*. Texas: University of Texas Press.

Saussure, F. de. (1986). *Course in General Linguistics.* Chicago: Open Court Publishing Company.

Stockwell, P. (2002). *Cognitive Poetics. An Introduction*. London: Routledge.

Stockwell, P. (2006). Schema Theory: Stylistic applications. In: K. Brown *et al.* (eds.). *Encyclopaedia of Language and Linguistics*. Amsterdam: Elseviere Science. 8–13.

Sturrock, J. (2003). *Structuralism*. Oxford: Blackwell.

Tabakowska, E. (1995). *Gramatyka i obrazowanie: Wprowadzenie do językoznawstwa kognitywnego*. Kraków: Wydawnictwo PAN.

*Mikołaj Deckert*
University of Łódź

# A NOTE ON TRANSLATION AND RELEVANCE

## 1. Introduction

Building on the ideas of Gutt (1998, 2000, 2004), this paper makes use of the advances of Relevance Theory (Sperber and Wilson 1986) to accommodate selected issues in Translation Studies. It attempts to demonstrate the impact that the consideration of relevance might have on the decision-making process of translation. A further matter considered here is whether translation is always to be seen as governed solely by the principles of intralingual communication.

## 2. Relevance: contextual effects vs. processing effort

Relevance Theory offers a novel cognitively-oriented theoretical foundation to account for the rules underlying human communication. Sperber and Wilson (1986: 122) state that "an assumption is relevant in a context if and only if it has some contextual effect in that context." Yet, as they go on to expound, relevance is a matter of degree which generally depends upon a trade-off between the contextual effects obtained by processing an input and the effort spent in the process.

The cognitive principle of relevance, one of the central tenets of Relevance Theory, holds that "human cognition tends to be geared towards the maximisation of relevance" (Sperber and Wilson 1986: 260). Thus, the addressees expect the stimuli produced by the sender to provide them with positive contextual/cognitive effects without forcing them to spend more energy than is necessary on processing the stimuli. This suggests that, if acquiring a piece of information is too costly compared to the cognitive benefits it brings, the audience should be spared any effort whatsoever.

## 3. Cognitive environment and context

Relevance Theory also sheds new light on the old concept of context. The notion extends beyond "information about the immediate physical environment or the immediately preceding utterances" (Sperber and Wilson 1986: 15) to include a wide range of elements such as "expectations about the future, scientific hypotheses or religious beliefs, anecdotal memories, general cultural assumptions, beliefs about the mental state of the speaker." The term 'context' is sometimes used interchangeably with the term 'cognitive environment' (of an individual) which is defined as "a set of facts that are manifest [perceivable or inferable] to him" (Sperber and Wilson 1986: 15–16), even though context is strictly speaking a subset within a particular cognitive environment.

## 4. Secondary communication

It goes without saying that the interlocutors' contexts are often incompatible. Gutt (2000) talks of secondary communication situations, i.e. circumstances in which the cognitive environments of audiences are devoid of the contextual assumptions to be utilised in the comprehension procedure.

The pursuit of optimal relevance in secondary communication situations, still within a single language, can be illustrated by means of the following example. Consider an exchange between two MA students, a part of which proceeds as follows:

Speaker 1: What is your thesis about?
Speaker 2: It's about translation and Relevance Theory. [Utterance 1]

At this point the Speaker 1's cognitive environment enters into an interaction with the linguistic evidence provided in the form of the answer. If Speaker 1, taken to have some knowledge about translation, has access to a sufficient number of assumptions about Relevance Theory, she can derive an interpretation and gain contextual effects which might include the following:

Inference 1: The thesis will be theoretical to a large extent;
Inference 2: Speaker 2 needed/needs/will need to get acquainted with the tenets of Relevance Theory;
Inference 3: To write about Relevance Theory in the context of translation, Speaker 2 will relate to the deliberations of Ernst-August Gutt;
Inference 4: The dissertation will not be exclusively based on the code model of communication.

Needless to say, the network of associations activated by Utterance 1 can be further developed, the limit being only the receptor's knowledge, her processing capabilities and the degree of relevance she finds satisfactory in the communicative situation.

But one could just as well imagine that Speaker 1 is ignorant about Relevance Theory. In such a case, the interpretation would not proceed so smoothly. Leaving aside the fact that the response could create a picture of Speaker 2 being cocky or condescending, such an answer would cause puzzlement for Speaker 1, as the link between her cognitive environment and the data provided by Speaker 2 would be weak if not non-existent. She would be incapable of accessing relevant contextual assumptions to be used in processing the utterance, and her expectations of relevance would not be satisfied. The contextual effects in this case would most probably be limited to concluding that a sizeable part of the thesis is going to be theoretical (as the word 'theory' is explicitly given in the answer) and that it is going to be about translation. Yet, the rather paltry modification of Speaker 1's representation of the world would have been brought about at the cost of disproportionately large processing effort.

In view of that reservation, the answer can be reformulated and the exchange may proceed in the following manner:

Speaker 1: What is your thesis about?
Speaker 2: It's a theoretical piece on translation. [Utterance 2]

In this instance the obtainable contextual effects are roughly the same as in the previous case. However, it is crucial here that the mental effort spent on acquiring those effects is significantly less since Speaker 1 is spared the superfluous puzzlement incurred by the original reply (Utterance 1) and does not consume energy browsing her mental encyclopaedia in vain. Though the intrinsic informative value of the response is smaller than that of the original one, the balance of processing effort versus contextual effects is more favourable in this exchange and hence the answer is more relevant to Speaker 1, whose cognitive environment lacks the assumptions necessary for processing the more specific answer.

The correlation between cognitive environments and derivable interpretations may be mapped in the manner shown in Figure 1, adapted from Gutt (2004):

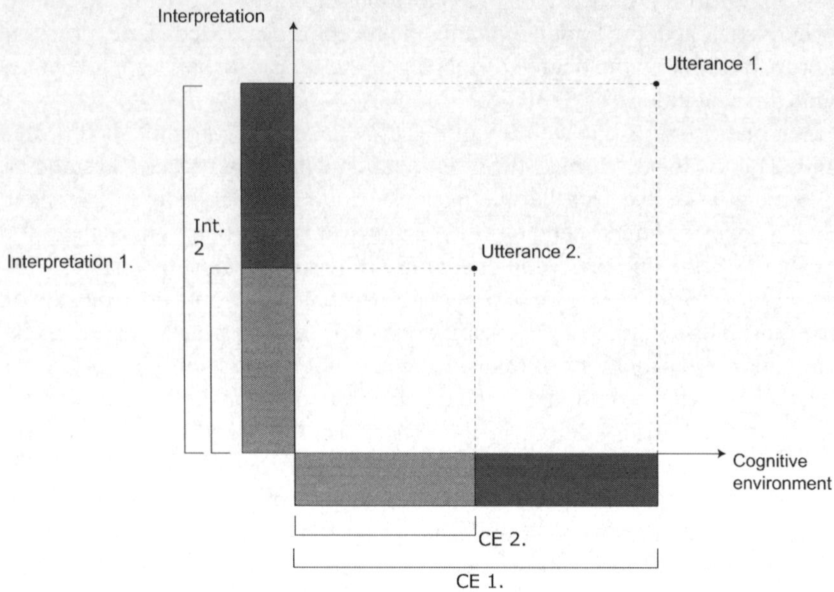


Fig. 1. Cognitive environment and interpretation (Gutt 2004)

## 5. Relevance in translation

Secondary communication situations are not uncommon in translation. The audiences' cognitive environments tend to be dissimilar, as are their socio-cultural milieux. This obstacle might be surmounted in several ways. According to Gutt (2004), the following solutions are available: (1) to adjust the receptors' cognitive environments so that the originally-intended interpretation becomes comprehensible; (2) to adjust the interpretation to be communicated in such a way that it can be comprehended within the receptors' current cognitive environments; or (3) to adjust both the receptors' cognitive environments and the intended interpretation.

In the student exchange example, the problem of secondary communication was alleviated by dispensing with the unintelligible component, which approximates solution (2). Omission or a hypernym is an option for the translator, too. In the case of operative texts (Reiss 1971/2004, 1976), for example where the source-text function (eliciting a particular response) is crucially to be transmitted, a way out is to replace the problematic term with an element which could serve the intended target-text purpose.[1] Thus, the original semantic content

[1] However, the functions of the ST and the TT may be different in their respective cultures.

Venuti's (1995: 18) argument against fluent translation, "it is the forcible replacement of the linguistic and cultural difference of the foreign text" and "whatever difference the translation conveys is (...) imprinted by the target-language culture, assimilated to its positions and intelligibility."[4]

To get a clearer picture, let us take a look at an example from Antoni Libera's *Madame*.[5] At one point, conjecturing about the eponymous woman, the narrator-protagonist refers to a location in Warsaw called 'MDM' ['Marszałkowska Dzielnica Mieszkaniowa']. Translation-wise it poses a problem because the acronym, denoting a social realist housing estate, is strictly culture-specific (set in communist Poland in the 1960s, the novel as such is a rather meticulous account of the realia). The translator can then choose to render 'MDM' verbatim along the lines of 'Marshal's Residential District.' A different solution is to employ a footnote, although this could be regarded a translational failure by many translation theorists. Another possibility is to explicitate the concept and this is what Agnieszka Kołakowska does in the official rendition. Her English text turns 'arkady MDM-u' into 'the arcades of that other lugubrious 1950s monolith, the Young People's Housing District,' which is evidently additive to make allowances for the potential gaps in the receptors' knowledge. In the case of *Madame*, opting for the functionally-oriented procedures akin to domestication seems out of the question since it would distort the original not only by depriving it of its socio-historical flavour, but vitally by giving the readers a forged flavour in its stead. Interestingly, as was confirmed in an in-class discussion among literary translation students, few translators would venture to replant 'MDM' into the target text. Leaving the foreign constituent intact would be found fault with by virtue of the fact that non-Polish readers are very unlikely to know how it is to be interpreted. In relevance-theoretic

[4] To support the claim one could think of the following analogy: since translations are predominantly renderings of texts embedded in extrinsic cultures, there seems to be a kind of parallel between visiting foreign countries and reading translated text. In this vein, if one hosts a visitor from another country, say Italy, it seems *de rigueur* to acquaint the guest with the customs typical of one's household, city or country, in our hypothetical case, Poland. Of course, the host might be eager to learn from the visitor about his 'cultural territory,' but the flow of culturally new stimuli will be mostly targeted at the guest. (S)he will be the one to find his or her way in the new setting, including language. The essence of travelling is, I believe, to come into contact with new entities and phenomena which conventionally could be referred to as 'culture' (cf. also Newmark 1988, 2001). Therefore, it would be unreasonable to expect the host to adjust her lifestyle entirely so as to spare the visitor the confusion of contact with the unknown; and the Italian guest would rightly be startled if his host were to serve only typically Italian dishes not giving him/her a chance to get any idea of the flavour of traditional Polish cuisine. Such a visit, in the sense of physical travelling or, less literally, progressing through a translation, would be unlikely to expand the visitor's knowledge or enrich his or her experience. Vitally, helpful as the analogy is, it need not follow that it is futile reading untranslated from one's own cultural background.

[5] The disclaimer here is that it would be a misconception to see literary texts as confined to their communicative layer.

terms, by choosing the unfamiliar item rather than by, for example undertranslating (Newmark 1981), the translator would consciously and purposefully give to the audience a variant that incurs additional processing effort upon them and therefore is not optimally relevant.[6]

This is not to claim that equating translation with intralingual communication is invariably erroneous since the validity of such an equation depends on several translational constraints,[7] such as text type (Reiss 1971/2004, 1976) and function, *skopos* of the text (Vermeer 1978, 1983) or audience design (Bell 1984).[8] Palpably, in reaching for a translation of a historical novel readers have different expectations than when attempting to get a TV set started and making recourse to a manual. Similarly, a translation of a cartoon for children is unlikely to be taken to task for prioritising TT effect over ST semantic content to ensure interpretability for the young audience.[9]

## 6. Conclusions

All in all, by refusing to treat efficiency as the prime concern, interlingual (and cross-cultural) intentional information transmission can be taken to be partially at loggerheads with the conventionally-seen communication.

It thus follows that the translator should take nothing for granted and should not endeavour to achieve comprehensibility of the TT at the cost of effacing the foreign from the ST and adjusting the input to the receptors' cognitive environments.[10] And this is the tendency that, though criticised in passing (cf. Venuti 1995, 1998; Berman 1985/2004), has held sway in translation for a few decades now.[11]

Therefore, it is argued here that before embarking on a translation task the translator ought to ask himself or herself whether the cultural otherness is to be

[6] The question arises if in the case of monolingual/monocultural communication, the situation is still that of primary communication sort. If not, optimisation of comprehension for the target audience could put them in a more comfortable position than the source audience are.

[7] However, Gutt (1990: 1) maintains that translational phenomena "can be accounted for without recourse to typologies of texts, translations, functions or the like."

[8] Another important factor is the form of transmission. Oral communication is generally more immediate, the time the audience have at their disposal to process the input is shorter than in the case of written texts, which can usually be processed at a pace to suit the individual. This has a strong bearing on interpretation and audiovisual translation. Moreover, in those two modes some strictly technical constraints are at play.

[9] Still, some consumers of cartoons, such as Western fans of Japanese *anime*, might actively be seeking the exotic.

[10] Plainly, cultural distance is merely one of the lenses through which the problem of (not) making the TT maximally accessible can be analysed.

[11] For example Nida (1964/2004: 157) contends that „during the past fifty years (...) there has been a marked shift of emphasis from the formal to the dynamic dimension."

valorized or negated, transported or transformed.[12] Opting for the former could mean an additional expenditure of the audience's processing energy (in the form of initial confusion but also, more generally, consulting sources, etc.) and would prevent the signal from being optimally relevant. Importantly, any audience reasoning in line with the communicative principle of relevance (Sperber and Wilson 1986: 158) could be misled.[13]

## References

Bell, A. (1984). Language style and audience design. *Language in Society* 13: 145–204.

Berman, A. (1985/2004). Translation and the trials of the foreign. In: L. Venuti (ed.). 276–289.

Cicero, M. T. (46 BC/1960). De optimo genere oratorum. In: *De inventione; De optimo genere oratorum; Topica*. Cambridge, MA: Harvard University Press; London: Heinemann. 347–373.

Gutt, E.-A. (1990). *A theoretical account of translation – without a translation theory. Target* 2: 135–164.

Gutt, E-A. (1998). Pragmatic aspects of translation: some Relevance Theory observations.
In: L. Hickey (ed.). *The Pragmatics of Translation*. Clevedon: Multilingual Matters.

Gutt, E.-A. (2000). *Translation and Relevance: Cognition and Context*. Manchester: St. Jerome.

Gutt, E.-A. (2004). Relevance Theory and translation: toward a new realism in Bible translation. Paper presented at *International Meeting of the Society of Biblical Literature*. Groningen, Netherlands.

House, J. (1977/1981). *A Model for Translation Quality Assessment*. Tübingen: Gunter Narr.

Levy, J. (1967/1989). Translation as a decision process. In: A. Chesterman (ed.). *Readings in Translation Theory*. Helsinki: Oy Finn Lectura Ab. 37–52.

Newmark, P. (1981). *Approaches to Translation*. Oxford and New York: Pergamon Press.

Newmark, P. (1988). *A Textbook of Translation*. New York and London: Prentice Hall.

Newmark, P. (2001). Translation and Culture. In: B. Lewandowska-Tomaszczyk and M. Thelen (eds.). *Translation and Meaning*. Part 5. *Proceedings of the Maastricht Session of the Third International Maastricht–Łódź Duo Colloquim on 'Translation and Meaning'*. Maastricht: Hogeschool Zuyd/Maastricht School of Translation and Interpreting. 327–334.

Nida, E. A. (1964). *Towards a Science of Translating*. Leiden: E. J. Brill.

Nida, E. A. (1964/2004). Principles of Correspondence. In: L. Venuti (ed.). 153–167.

Nord, C. (1991). *Text Analysis in Translation: Theory, Methodology and Didactic Application of a Model for Translation-Oriented Text Analysis*. Amsterdam: Rodopi.

Reiss, K. (1971/2004). Type, kind and individuality of text: decision making in translation. In: L. Venuti (ed.). 168–179.

[12] In other words, the question is whether to treat an Italian visitor to pork chop and cabbage or to lasagna bolognese (see note 4).

[13] In introducing the principle of relevance, Sperber and Wilson (1986: 158) explain that „every act of ostensive communication communicates the presumption of its own optimal relevance." This principle is subsequently labelled the communicative principle of relevance to distinguish it from the cognitive principle of relevance (see section 2).

Reiss, K. (1976). *Texttyp und Übersetzungsmethode: Der operative Text*. Kronberg: Scriptor Verlag.
Rieu, E. V. , Philips, J. B. (1954). Translating the Gospels. *Bible Translator* 6: 150–159.
Schleiermacher, F. (1813/2004). On the different methods of translating. In: L. Venuti (ed.). 43–63.
Sperber, D., Wilson, D. (1986). *Relevance: Communication and Cognition*. Oxford: Blackwell.
Toury, G. (1995). *Descriptive Translation Studies – And Beyond*. Amsterdam and Philadelphia, PA: John Benjamins.
Venuti, L. (1995). *The Translator's Invisibility: A History of Translation*. London and New York: Routledge.
Venuti, L. (1998). *The Scandals of Translation: Towards an Ethics of Difference*. London: Routledge.
Venuti, L. (2004). (ed.). *The Translation Studies Reader*, 2nd ed., London: Routledge.
Vermeer, H. J. (1978). Ein Rahmen für eine allgemeine Translationstheorie. *Lebende Sprachen* 23: 99–102.
Vermeer, H. J. (1983). *Aufsätze zur Translationstheorie*. Heidelberg: Selbstverlag.

*Dobromiła Jagiełła*
Jagiellonian University, Kraków

# ON THE SYNTACTIC AND NON-SYNTACTIC ASPECTS OF THE GRAMMAR OF ANAPHORS AND PRONOUNS

## 1. Introduction

This paper takes a close look at the referential properties of nominal phrases and the conditions which govern the necessary or possible anaphoric dependencies between different NPs in a sentence. Two main perspectives on the phenomenon, both grounded within formal, generative studies on language, are investigated here. The first one is Chomsky's (1981, 1986) classic model, in which the conditions on the distribution and interpretation of referentially dependent expressions are syntactic in nature. The second is Pollard and Sag's (1992) model, in which the relevant binding conditions are separated into syntactic and non-syntactic. The latter model has strongly influenced the recent rival Binding Theory (BT) of Culicover and Jackendoff (2005). Since the main language of illustration in the above-mentioned accounts is English, Polish has been examined here to verify the theoretical claims empirically against a broader range of data.

## 2. Essentials of binding

Consider the paradigmatic binding contrast observed in a wide variety of languages, illustrated in (1) and (2) with examples from English:

(1) John$_i$ likes him$_{*i/j}$.
(2) John$_i$ likes himself$_{i/*j}$.

The most natural interpretation of the sentence in (1) is that *John* and *him* cannot be coreferential, i.e., these two NPs cannot designate the same person. In an approach that captures the referential properties of NPs with indices, referential co-identity and referential distinctness can be captured as shown in (3). Under (3), *John* and *him* cannot bear the same index in (1) and therefore, the NPs can only be interpreted as disjoint in reference (Lasnik and Uriagereka 1988: 45):

(3) a. If two NPs have the same index, they are *coreferential.*
b. If two NPs have different indices, they are *disjoint in reference.*

In contrast to (1), *John* and *himself* in (2) must be coreferential. In the generative paradigm, NPs like *him, her, my*, etc. are referred to as pronouns; reflexive NPs such as *himself, herself, myself*, etc. and reciprocal NPs *each other* and *one another* are categorized as anaphors. What the contrast between (1) and (2) indicates is that anaphors must pick their reference from antecedents while pronouns need not and sometimes must not have antecedents in the syntactic structures in which they occur. In (1) above, the pronoun *him* is most likely to pick its referent from an entity salient in the larger situational contexts in which (1) is uttered, e.g. *Peter*, in the context in which (1), repeated below as (4b), is a response to (4a):

(4) a. And what about Peter$_j$?
b. John$_i$ likes him$_{*i/j}$.

As *him* is most likely to be perceived as coreferential with *Peter* in (4), the interpretation of (4b) derives from the use of the sentence for communicative purposes and it arises in a pragmatically specific context (Haegeman 1998: 204). By contrast, the interpretation of reflexives like *himself* in (2) is determined grammatically.

To wrap up, it might be stated that the interpretation of referentially dependent NPs is controlled by semantic and/or pragmatic principles. Nevertheless, the contrast between (1) and (2) shows that the distribution and interpretation of anaphors and pronouns is constrained by syntactic constraints as well. This observation has been made in formal studies of a wide variety of languages (Chomsky 1981, 1986). First, with regard to contexts like the ones in (1) and (2), it might be concluded that anaphors and pronouns are in complementary distribution in the syntactic structures in which they occur, i.e., where pronouns can occur, anaphors cannot, and vice versa. Secondly, anaphor-binding and pronominal disjoint reference hold within a local domain, as demonstrated in (5):

(5) a. Bill$_i$ thinks that John$_j$ likes himself$_{*i/j}$.
b. Bill$_i$ thinks that John$_j$ likes him$_{i/*j}$.
c. Bill$_i$ hopes that *himself$_i$/he$_i$ will win.
d. Bill$_i$ believed Kate to be likely to praise *himself$_i$/him$_i$.

The syntactic binding conditions on anaphors and pronouns are captured informally in Lasnik and Uriagereka (1988: 31) as shown in (6), where 'nearby' stands for some minimal syntactic domain in which binding conditions must be satisfied:

(6) a. An anaphor must have an antecedent nearby.
b. A pronominal must not have an antecedent nearby.

In Chomsky's model of generative grammar, the grammatically determined aspects of the distribution and interpretation of anaphors and pronouns occurring in syntactic structures are underpinned by three crucial formal concepts: c-command, locality, and obligatoriness. These concepts are discussed in some below.

## 3. The formal treatment of c-command, locality, and obligatoriness of anaphor-binding

### 3.1. C-command

On the basis of the examples discussed so far, it might be assumed that an anaphor is bound if it is coindexed with an NP in some local domain. However, if this were the case, the ungrammaticality of (7b) would not be ruled out:

(7) a. John$_i$ likes himself$_{i/*j}$.
b. *John's$_i$ mother likes himself$_i$.

The impossibility of the NP *John* to serve as the antecedent for the anaphor in (7b) is taken as evidence that the syntactic relation between them is of the wrong type, in contrast to (7a). Specifically, the antecedent must *c-command* the anaphor, where c-command is defined as in (8) below:

(8) C-command:
A node A c-commands a node B iff:
A does not dominate B;
B does not dominate A;
the first branching node dominating A also dominates B.

(9) a. b.

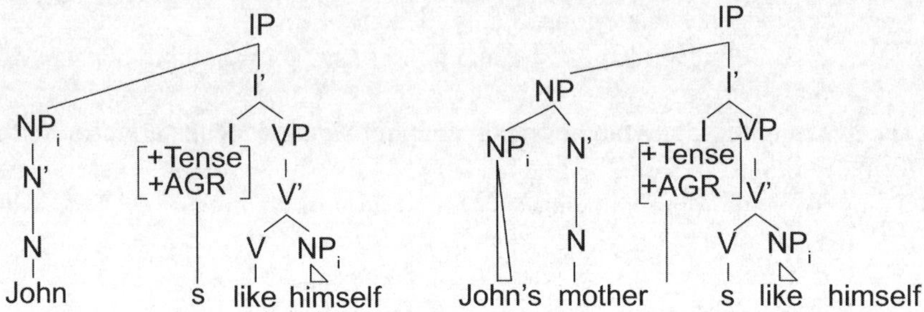


To capture the structural difference between the coindexed NPs in the examples (7a) and (7b), the relation of *binding* might be defined as follows:

(10) A binds B iff:
A c-commands B;
A and B are coindexed.

The diagrams in (10a) and (10b), which represent the structure of (7a) and (7b), respectively, clearly demonstrate that the NP *John* binds the reflexive in (7a) but not in (7b).
The binding condition on anaphors can thus be stated as in (11). To capture the complementarity of the distribution of anaphors and pronouns, the binding condition on pronouns in (12) can be posited alongside:

(11) An anaphor must be bound nearby.
(12) A pronominal must be free nearby.

### 3.2. Locality

Having clarified the formal aspect of the binding relation and introduced the binding conditions, it seems necessary to investigate the exact boundaries of the binding domain, by which a local domain within which an anaphor must and a pronoun cannot find its antecedent is understood. Chomsky (1981, 1986) suggests that binding is a local structural relation and that it is restricted to two categories, NP and IP. The relevance of the domain of NP for binding can be illustrated with the examples in (13):

(13) a. Ann$_i$ heard [$_{NP}$ stories about herself$_i$].
b. Ann$_i$ heard [$_{NP}$ Kate$_j$'s stories about her$_{i/*j}$/herself$_{*i/j}$].

As can be observed in (13), an anaphor may look for its antecedent outside the including NP provided this NP does not have a potential binder in the specifier position [Spec, NP] that functions as the subject of the larger NP. Otherwise, an anaphor must be bound within its NP. This syntactic constraint is known as the *Specified Subject Condition* (SSC) (Chomsky 1973), and it is formulated in (14) below:

(14) The Specified Subject Condition (SSC):
X may not bind Y in the structure:
$\ldots X \ldots [_{\alpha} \ldots Z \ldots W_1 Y W_2 \ldots] \ldots$
where Z is the subject of $W_1 Y W_2$.

(14) accounts for both (13b) and (5d) above, as *Kate* is a specified subject that prevents anaphoric dependence between an external or outside antecedent and an embedded anaphor.

As noted before, IP counts as a proper binding domain for anaphors as well. However, the statement that an anaphor must be bound in the smallest IP in which it is included calls for some refinement in view of the sentence in (15a), which is grammatical in contrast to (15b):

(15) a. $\text{Kate}_i$ believes $[_{IP}$ $\text{herself}_i$ to be a hard-working student].
b. *$\text{Kate}_i$ believes [that $[_{IP}$ $\text{herself}_i$ is a hard-working student]].

The difference between (15a) and (15b) is that in the former the antecedent and the anaphor are in the same minimal domain of tense. In (15b), on the other hand, the antecedent and the anaphor are not in the same minimal tensed clause. The condition that blocks anaphor-binding from extending beyond the minimal domain of tense (15b) is the *Tensed Sentence Condition* (TSC) of Chomsky (1973), which is defined in (16) below:

(16) The Tensed Sentence Condition (TSC):
X cannot bind Y in the structure:
$\ldots X \ldots [_{\alpha} \ldots Y \ldots] \ldots$ where $\alpha$ is a tensed clause.

### 3.3. Obligatoriness

The third essential property that characterizes anaphor-binding is obligatoriness: an anaphor must be bound. That every anaphor must have a coindexed, c-commanding antecedent NP within its binding domain (i.e., the minimal NP with a specified subject or the minimal containing tensed IP) is manifested by the following contrasts:

(17) a. *Himself will win.
b. He will win.

(18) a. *Pictures of himself will be on sale.
b. Pictures of him will be on sale.
(19) a. *It seemed to himself that he would win.
b. It seemed to him that he would win.

## 4. Problems

The classic BT of Chomsky (1981, 1986) has not gone unchallenged. Several subsequent generative studies of the phenomenon have shown the three crucial properties that play a role in determining the distribution of anaphors and pronouns in syntactic structures to be problematic, as is briefly discussed below.

### 4.1. C-command

Pollard and Sag (1992), henceforth P&S, have drawn attention to reflexives embedded in NPs headed by so-called picture nouns, which seem to have special properties that distinguish them from ordinary reflexives. Namely, although the anaphors in (20) and (21) fail to be c-commanded within their minimal binding domains, the sentences are grammatical, contrary to the predictions of the syntactic condition on anaphor-binding. Therefore, P&S have postulated that such anaphors should be exempt from the syntactic constraints on binding:

(20) $[_{NP}$ Nude pictures of herself$_i$] do not offend Mary$_i$.
(21) $[_{NP}$ Pictures of himself$_i$] excite John$_i$.

However, the problem posed by examples like (20) and (21) need not be a serious counterexample to the syntactic approach to binding conditions. In particular, the anaphors in (20) and (21) can be analyzed as bound in their binding domains assuming a Larsonian analysis of the structure of VP (Larson 1988: 366–68).

First, observe that the sentences in (20) – (21) include so-called psych-verbs, such as *offend*, *excite*, *worry*, *annoy*, *frighten*, *please*, etc. It seems that the subject of a psych-verb can contain a reflexive coreferential with the object NP, which is not possible with genuine transitives. The surface object of a psych-verb behaves like the subject of a transitive clause with respect to anaphoric dependencies in that it can bind an anaphor embedded within the surface subject. Thus, we might expect that at some level of syntactic derivation the surface psych-verb object c-commands the surface subject. For (21), Larson (1988) proposes the analysis given in (22) below:

(22)

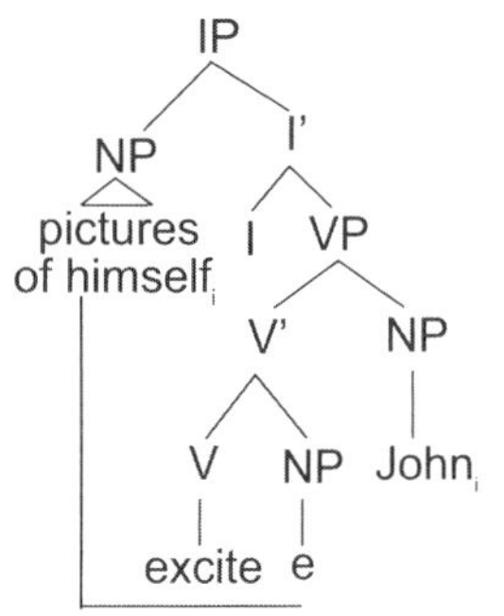


The basic idea here is that psych-verbs are unaccusatives with two internal arguments. The verb *excite* fails to assign Case to *pictures of himself* and it also fails to assign an external theta role. This forces movement to subject position, as indicated. In the resulting structure the surface subject is a derived subject. Furthermore, it attains its position from a site lower than the surface object. Turning to the surface object, it is in fact a structural (VP) subject – the most prominent theta-marked argument in the theta grid of the verb. It c-commands and hence binds the anaphor in the NP which is the verb's sister prior to movement, which explains why the binding condition on anaphors is satisfied in (22). In this scenario, anaphors found in NPs containing picture nouns are not exempt from the syntactic binding conditions.

### 4.2. Locality

P&S have also argued against the locality constraint on anaphor-binding. According to them, the coindexing in (23) is not absolute and should not be enforced by the principles of grammar but rather, by some processing (*intervention*) constraints. Substituting the intervening NP *Tom* (which functions as the antecedent for the anaphor) with an inanimate NP improves the acceptability of picture noun reflexives coindexed with non-local antecedents, as shown in (24). For P&S, this proves that the extension of the local domain should not be captured under syntactically-determined constraints. Similar effects arise in the context of quantified and expletive intervenors, as demonstrated in (25):

(23) Bill$_j$ remembered that Tom$_i$ saw [a picture of himself$_{i/*j}$] in the post office.

(24) a. ?Bill$_i$ remembered that *The Times* had printed [a picture of himself$_i$] in the Sunday edition.

b. $Bill_i$ suspected that the silence meant that [a picture of $himself_i$] would
soon be on the post office wall.

(25) a. $Bill_i$ thought that *nothing* could make [a picture of $himself_i$ in *The Times*] acceptable to Sandy.
b. $Bill_i$ knew that *it* would take [a picture of $himself_i$ with Hilary Clinton] to get Sandy's attention.

Furthermore, the nature of the determiner introducing an NP containing an anaphor seems to affect acceptability of long-distance binding. For example, changing the determiner in (24a) to *the* or *that* to make the phrase more definite tends to enhance the acceptability of such examples, as shown in (26) below:

(26) What $Bill_i$ finally realized was that *The Times* was going to print [*that* picture of $himself_i$ with Hilary Clinton] in the Sunday edition.

Following Kuno (1987), P&S take the reflexives in (23) – (26) to be licensed by the *point of view* principle, which is pragmatic rather than syntactic in nature. In other words, reflexives, particularly exempt picture noun reflexives illustrated in (23) – (26), fall outside the syntactic binding condition on anaphors and are assigned the antecedent whose viewpoint or perspective is represented in the text/larger linguistic and/or situational context. Such reflexives are analyzed by Kuno (1987) not as anaphors, but as *logophors*. The logophoric nature of some reflexives can be illustrated with the contrast in (27) from Kuno (1987: 164):

(27) a. $John_i$ knows that there is a picture of $himself_i$ in the morning paper.
b. * $John_i$ still doesn't know that there is a picture of $himself_i$ in the morning paper.

In (27b), himself is not a logophor, since if John is not in the requisite internal state, the reflexive cannot represent his perspective, unlike in (27a). Generally speaking, logophoric contexts are sentences with verbs of communication and mental state (e.g. tell, know, expect, etc.) and with psych-predicates (e.g. worry, disturb, please, etc.), whose experiencer arguments generate the point of view perspective on the situation. Notice that the reflexives in (27) lack antecedents in their local binding domain. For Kuno (1987) as well as for P&S, they are exempt from the syntactic part of BT. The reflexive in (27a) is licensed pragmatically under the point of view principle, while the reflexive in (27b) is not.

### 4.3. Obligatoriness

Finally, P&S have also pointed out the existence of discourse-bound reflexives in English, which violate the syntactic BT of Chomsky (1981, 1986) by not being bound in their binding domains:

(28) a. Mary$_i$ was extremely upset. That picture of herself$_i$ on the front page of *The Times* would circulate all over the world.
b. John$_i$ was going to get even with Mary. That picture of himself$_i$ in the paper would annoy her.

## 5. Implicit antecedents

As stated earlier, the BT formulated in Chomsky (1981, 1986) predicts that pronouns and anaphors are in complementary distribution. However, the predicted complementarity breaks down in certain circumstances. Consider (29):

(29) a. John$_i$ likes [$_{NP}$ Bill's stories about him$_i$/ *himself$_i$].
b. John$_i$ likes [$_{NP}$ stories about him$_i$].
c. John$_i$ likes [$_{NP}$ stories about himself$_i$].

Given that the binding domain is defined identically for pronouns and anaphors, (29c) poses a problem for BT, as the sentence is grammatical despite the fact that the anaphor is not bound in its binding domain (the minimal including NP). To account for the cases where complementarity breaks down, Chomsky (1986) redefines the binding domain as the smallest domain in which all the grammatical functions of the head *could* be satisfied; in essence, the binding domain of the anaphor is extended outside the containing NP to the domain of IP just in case there is no potential binder within the NP:

(30) Binding domain:
The binding domain for α is the minimal *Complete Functional Complex (CFC)* that contains α and a governor of α in which α's binding condition could, in principle, be satisfied.

Chomsky (1986) makes use of the notion 'potential binder,' i.e., an NP that c-commands an anaphor or a pronoun in the relevant domain. The presence or absence of a potential binder (in contrast to an actual binder) should have no effect on the condition on pronouns, since there is no requirement that a pronoun must be bound, i.e., that it must have a binder, in its binding domain. (29b) and (29c) are both licit under (30): in (29b) either there is no subject within the NP or there is a null subject interpreted as non-coreferential with *him*$_i$, hence the pronoun is free. For (29c), Chomsky (1986) assumes that the NP is not a CFC for the anaphor, as it lacks a potential binder. In this case, the clause is the minimal CFC for the anaphor and (29c) is grammatical in compliance with BT.

## 6. Splitting the Binding Theory: evidence from Polish

To find out whether it is well-motivated to divide the conditions on the distribution and interpretation of reflexives and pronouns into two distinct kinds: the syntactic, which are underpinned by the notions of c-command, locality and obligatoriness, and processing and pragmatic constraints, which are not sensitive to these properties, as has been argued for by P&S as well as by Culicover and Jackendoff (2005), henceforth C&J, the two theoretical stands on the nature of binding relations in natural language should be verified against a broader range of linguistic data, preferably from different languages. In particular, if P&S and C&J are right, we can expect to find the processing and pragmatic effects in a wide range of languages.

While Chomsky's (1981, 1986) account applies to data from Polish, indicating some parametric variation with respect to the SSC (cf. Willim 1989), both P&S's (1992) and C&J's (2005) models run into problems confronted with Polish data. First, both P&S and C&J predict that in a sentence like (31) the reflexive *sobie 'self'* is exempt from the syntactic part of BT:

(31) Jan$_i$ przeczytał [$_{NP}$ wszystkie artykuły o sobie$_i$/ *nim$_i$].
'John$_i$ read all the articles about (him)self$_i$/ him$_i$.'

Recall that P&S's argument against the syntactic nature of the binding condition on a reflexive included in an NP with a picture noun is based on its non-local character. Thus, if the reflexive in (31) is exempt from the syntactic part of BT, the binding relation is not expected to be constrained by locality and the anaphor can be expected to search freely for its antecedent outside the clause boundary. However, this is contrary to fact, as shown in (32):

(32) a. *Jan$_i$ upierał się, żeby przeczytane zostały wszystkie artykuły o sobie$_i$.
'John$_i$ insisted that all the articles about (him)self$_i$ should be read.'
b. *Jan$_i$ chciał, żeby opowieści o swoim$_i$ bracie okazały się wymyślone.
'John wanted the stories about his$_i$ (= self's$_i$) brother to turn out to have been made up.'

The fact that the anaphors in (32) cannot search for antecedents outside the minimal tensed clause suggests that picture noun reflexives should not be exempt from the syntactic constraints on binding. This is further verified by the fact that Polish does not license discourse-bound anaphors (cf. (28)):

(33) Jan$_i$ był wściekły. *[Swój$_i$ artykuł/ Artykuł o sobie$_i$] został skrytykowany.
'John$_i$ was furious.*[An article by (him)self$_i$/ about (him)self$_i$] had been criticized.'

Furthermore, Polish does not confirm P&S's prediction that anaphors embedded in picture NPs are sensitive to processing constraint effects, e.g. the prediction that introducing an inanimate intervener NP in a sentence or changing the determiner of a picture noun phrase to make it more definite improves the possibility of coindexing a picture noun reflexive with a non-local antecedent. There are no acceptability differences between (34) on the one hand and (36) – (37) on the other hand:

(34) Piotr$_i$ przypuszczał, że Jan$_j$ opublikuje [zdjęcia ze swojego$_{*i/j}$ koncertu].
'Peter$_i$ believed that John$_j$ would publish [pictures from his (= self's$_{i/j}$) concert].'

(35) Piotr$_i$ przypuszczał, że Jan$_j$ opublikuje [tamto zdjęcie ze swojego$_{*i/j}$ koncertu].
'Peter$_i$ believed that John$_j$ would publish [that picture from his (= self's$_{i/j}$) concert].'

(36) Piotr$_i$ nie wierzył, że *Newsweek* opublikuje [*zdjęcia ze swojego$_i$ koncertu].
'Peter$_i$ did not believe that *Newsweek* would release [*pictures from his (= self's$_i$) concert].'

(37) Piotr$_i$ bał się, że cisza oznacza, że [*to zdjęcie ze swojego$_i$ koncertu] zatrzęsie opinią publiczną.
'Peter$_i$ was afraid that silence meant that [that picture from his (= self's$_i$) concert] would shock the public opinion.'

Finally, Polish offers rather restricted evidence for the existence of (point of view) logophors in structures with psych-predicates:

(38) a. ??[Artykuły o swoich$_i$ programach] usatysfakcjonowały polityków$_i$.
'[The articles about their (= selves'$_i$) programs] satisfied the politicians$_i$.'
b. ?? [Zdjęcia ze swoich$_i$ ostatnich wystąpień] zirytowały polityków$_i$.
'[The pictures from their (= selves'$_i$) latest public appearances] irritated the politicians$_i$.'

In conclusion, the empirical data from Polish analyzed here indicate that exempting picture noun reflexives from the syntactic conditions on binding and splitting BT into the syntactic and non-syntactic part is not well-grounded. At the same time, the Polish data raise questions about the origin of non-local, especially pragmatically-bound anaphors, in language and their proper characterization in the theory of language.

## References

Chomsky, N. (1973). Conditions on transformations. In: S.R. Anderson and P. Kiparsky (eds.). *A Festschrift for Morris Halle*. New York: Holt, Rinehart & Winston. 232–286.

Chomsky, N. (1981). *Lectures on Government and Binding*. Dordrecht: Foris.

Chomsky, N. (1986). *Knowledge of Language*. New York: Praeger.

Culicover, P. W., Jackendoff, R. (2005). *Simpler Syntax*. Oxford: Oxford University Press.

Haegeman, L. (1998). *Introduction to Government and Binding Theory*. Oxford: Blackwell.

Kuno, S. (1987). *Functional Syntax: Anaphora, Discourse and Empathy*. Chicago: University of Chicago Press.

Larson, R. K. (1988). On the double object construction. *Linguistic Inquiry* 19 (3): 335–391.

Lasnik, H., Uriagereka, J. (1988). *A Course in GB Syntax: Lectures on Binding and Empty Categories*. Cambridge, Mass.: MIT Press.

Pollard, C., Sag, I. A. (1992). Anaphors and the scope of Binding Theory. *Linguistic Inquiry* 23: 261–303.

Willim, E. (1989). *On Word Order: A Government-Binding Study of English and Polish*. Kraków: Wydawnictwo Uniwersytetu Jagiellońskiego.

*Marek Majer*
University of Łódź

# HOW MANY GRAMMATICAL CASES WERE THERE IN PROTO-GERMANIC? INTERPRETING THE OLD ENGLISH EVIDENCE

## 1. Introduction

How many cases were there in Proto-Germanic (PG)? This question may most probably never be answered with certainty, as our knowledge of the language relies solely on linguistic reconstruction. However, it seems that we should be able to say relatively much about Proto-Germanic, as the comparative grammar of its daughter languages, the various Germanic dialects, has been studied extremely thoroughly in the course of the development of historical linguistics. Therefore, despite the fact that the question is not crucial, in this paper, I will attempt to establish the most probable answer.

The notion of Proto-Germanic is by no means unambiguous; in fact, the term may be used in reference to any stage of linguistic development later than Proto-Indo-European (PIE) and earlier than the rise of the distinct Germanic dialects. As regards the case system, it is quite certain that numerous processes must have taken place during this lengthy period. The aim is, therefore, to determine the number of grammatical cases in the final stage of the development of Proto-Germanic, i.e., the latest reconstructable stage from which all the attested Germanic languages may be derived. This implies that if a particular value of the category of case is not found in any of the attested dialects and no indications exist that it may have been part of the case system in the proto-language, it is assumed that it was not.[1]

[1] Of course, this methodology has clear disadvantages. For example, by conducting a comparative analysis of the modern Romance languages, one would never arrive at the inflectional system of Latin. Nevertheless, I regard this problem to be an inevitable and acceptable margin of error intrinsic to historical-comparative linguistics.

## 2. The Germanic case system: evidence from outside Old English

The attested Germanic dialects immediately point to the existence of at least six cases in PG: nominative ([N]), vocative ([V]), accusative ([AC]), genitive ([G]), dative ([D]), and instrumental ([I]) (Krahe 1942: 7, Bammesberger 1990: 12) . None of the languages displays the system in its entirety. [N] [G] [D] and [AC] are altogether unproblematic, since they survive to the present day in many languages, e.g. German and Icelandic. [V] is to be found only in Gothic (GOTH), where empirical evidence is scarce but undeniable; it was lost in West Germanic (WG) as well as in North Germanic (NG).[2] As regards [I], it is only attested in WG as a separate case, but this of course implies its existence in Proto-Germanic as well.[3]

On the other hand, the reconstructed PIE system is believed to have encompassed at least two further cases: locative ([L]) and ablative ([AB]). The best attestation of the assumed PIE system is found in Indo-Iranian. Naturally, it cannot be excluded that PIE actually had more cases, which we are not able to reconstruct. Conversely, it has also been suggested (Arumaa 1985: 112, Clackson 2007: 90, among others) that the declensional system of PIE was actually much simpler than what is usually reconstructed today and that a great deal of the complexities arose secondarily in the individual branches. Contrary to such objections, I believe that the richer system, even though it cannot be reconstructed perfectly, may be considered original for PIE or at least its late stages and that the less complex systems displayed by most of the daughter languages arose through simplification rather than through an expansion of a simpler archaic state.[4] In this scenario, the (late) PIE case system can be postulated to have had eight distinct members illustrated in Table 1 below with the masculine *o*-stem noun **u̯l̥k$^{w}$-o-* 'wolf' in the singular (cf. Ringe 2006: 49, Tichy 2004: 66):

---

[2] Incidentally, NG must have lost [V] by means of a morphological innovation (merger of [N] and [V] in favour of the former), as the distinction [N] **wulfaz* – [V] **wulf* would not have been obliterated by the application of the sound laws (Old Icelandic (OIc) [N] *ulfr* – [V] ***ulf*). In WG, on the other hand, the loss of [V] may have been purely phonetic: [N] **wulfaz* – [V] **wulf* both > Old English (OE) *wulf*, Old High German (OHG) *wolf* (Krahe 1942: 10).

[3] Such reasoning relies on the assumption that the number of cases could be reduced but not increased during the development of PG. Indeed, what we observe in the evolution of the Germanic languages is the loss of grammatical cases (Bammesberger 1990: 12). The reverse is extremely improbable; although such processes are attested in Indo-European (IE), most notably in Baltic and Tocharian, they are very rare and there are no indications whatsoever that Germanic should have expanded its case system at any point.

[4] Some scholars argue for a dialectal, not just chronological variation in this area; thus, the system in question would at least be original for the direct ancestor of Germanic and most branches of IE apart from Anatolian and Tocharian. For an overview of these hypotheses, see Clackson (2007: 9) and Fortson (2004: 9–11, 155).

Table 1. The case system of PIE (nominal declension)

| Case | Example |
|---|---|
| [N] | **u̯l̥kᵘ̯-o-s* |
| [G] | **u̯l̥kᵘ̯-o-s(i̯)o* |
| [D] | **u̯l̥kᵘ̯-o-ei̯* > **u̯l̥kᵘ̯-ōi̯* |
| [AC] | **u̯l̥kᵘ̯-o-m* |
| [I] | **u̯l̥kᵘ̯-o-*$h_1$ |
| [L] | **u̯l̥kᵘ̯-o/e-i̯* |
| [AB] | **u̯l̥kᵘ̯-o/e-ad* > **u̯l̥kᵘ̯-ād* |
| [V] | **u̯l̥kᵘ̯-e* |

It seems clear that the (late) PG case system must have represented an intermediate stage of development between the state displayed by PIE and that of the oldest attested Germanic languages. As stated above, this stage of development consisted in reducing the number of grammatical cases (Bammesberger 1990: 12). From a logical point of view, the possibilities are limited to four case systems distinguished with respect to the members that they include as well as their number. The possibilities are demonstrated in Table 2 below:

Table 2. Reconstructing the PG case system: theoretical possibilities

| PG case-system | [N] | [G] | [D] | [AC] | [I] | [L] | [AB] | [V] |
|---|---|---|---|---|---|---|---|---|
| a. | + | + | + | + | + | – | – | + |
| b. | + | + | + | + | + | + | – | + |
| c. | + | + | + | + | + | – | + | + |
| d. | + | + | + | + | + | + | + | + |

As for [N] [G] [D] [AC] [I], and [V], these cases seem unproblematic: they are all believed to have been present in PIE and are attested in the Germanic languages and can, therefore, be assumed to be inherited by PG. However, what must also be taken into account are complex morphological phenomena associated with case syncretism and potential functional shifts. As is well known, a particular morphological form realizing a set of morphosyntactic features (e.g. gender: masculine, number: singular, case: accusative) can in time be extended to realize a different set of morphosyntactic features (e.g. gender: masculine, number: singular, case: genitive), leading to the collapse of two (or more) morphosyntactic forms. This may be illustrated by the example, in (1) below, which shows the expansion of the exponence of [L] to [D]:

(1) (Post-)PIE *nok$^{u̯}$t-i*$_{F.SG.}$ 'night' ([L]) > Gk. νυκτ-ι$_{F.SG}$ ([D])

(Classical) Ancient Greek lost the PIE locative as a separate category, but in many declensional patterns the old locative forms were used to express the dative. In fact, the function of the 'dative' case in Ancient Greek is far wider than the traditional name of the category would imply, which is understandable, bearing in mind that it is descended from the PIE dative, locative and instrumental.

(2) PIE *u̯l̥k$^{u̯}$-e/o-ad* > *u̯l̥k$^{u̯}$ād*$_{M.SG}$. 'wolf' ([AB]) > Proto-Slavic (PSL) *vl̥'ka* > Polish (PL) *wilka*, Russian (RU) *волка* ([G])

Proto-Slavic lost the PIE ablative as a separate category (a merger with the genitive occurred), but in the singular of the *o*-stems, the old ablative form was retained to express the genitive: the widely attested modern Slavic ending *-a* is, therefore, an old ablative.

Similar phenomena may also be demonstrated for (Proto-)Germanic. As regards [N], [G], [D], [AC], [I], and [V], only [N] [G] [AC] [V] are completely unproblematic. Each reconstructable Germanic form may be directly traced back to its PIE counterpart, as shown in Table 3:

Table 3. The development of [N] [G] [AC] [V] from PIE to PG

| Case | PIE | PG |
|---|---|---|
| [N] | *u̯l̥k$^{u̯}$-o-s* | *wulf-az* |
| [G] | *u̯l̥k$^{u̯}$-o-s(i̯)o* | *wulf-asa* > *wulf-as*[5] |
| [AC] | *u̯l̥k$^{u̯}$-o-m* | *wulf-a*$^{N}$ |
| [V] | *u̯l̥k$^{u̯}$-e* | *wulf-e* > *wulf* |

[5] There is a number of serious phonological complications in tracing the development of this form (for example, some Germanic languages point to *-*as*, some to *-*es*), but that the PG ending is somehow descended from its PIE counterpart is quite certain (Must 1953, Bammesberger 1984).

The history of the remaining cases ([D] [I] [L] [AB]), however, seems to be much more complex. [D] and [I] are attested in the Germanic languages as separate cases, [L] and [AB] are not, but they are unlikely to have disappeared without a trace. Especially the Germanic [D] seems to represent the (partially?) merged PIE [D] and [L]. Numerous authors assume a complete merger of these categories already at the PG stage (Prokosch 1939: 235, Ringe 2006: 200). Syncretism with [I] frequently seems to go back to Proto-Germanic, at least in the plural. In fact, the details are so intricate that describing them here would be impossible, especially that various explanations have been proposed for many facts. Therefore, I will assume here a framework for all the developments outside Old English which is based primarily on Ringe (2006) and Boutkan (1995). In this framework, the developments that are considered valid are presented in (3):[6]

(3) The origin of the Germanic dative and instrumental forms:

a. North and West Germanic [D] of the *a*-stems (Early OE *-æ*, cf. Sievers--Brunner 1965: 195, Campbell 1959: 223; OHG *-e*, Runic (RUN) *-ai* > *-e*, Old Norse (ON) *-e*) in the singular may represent either the PIE [D] *-o-ei̯* or the [L] *-oi̯* , but *not* singular [I] in *-oh*$_1$ or *-eh*$_1$ (cf. below),

b. Gothic [D] of the *a*-stems (GOTH *-a*) may in the singular continue either PIE [L] *-oi̯* or [I] *-oh*$_1$ (perhaps *-eh*$_1$, originally a pronominal ending, cf. Tichy 2004: 67), but *not* the original singular [D] in *-ōi̯* < *-o-ei̯*,

c. Gothic, Old English and Old Saxon singular [D] of the *ō*-stems (GOTH. *-ai*, OE *-e*, OS *-a*/*-e*)[7] probably represents the PIE singular [D] *-eh*$_2$*ei̯*; singular [L] in *-eh*$_2$*i* is possible for OE and OS, but not for GOTH,

d. RUN, ON, OHG and Old Saxon (OS) singular [D] of the *ō*-stems (RUN *-u*, ON *-ø* with *u*-umlaut, OHG *-u*) continue the singular PIE [I] *-eh*$_2$*(e)h*$_1$,[8]

e. in the plural, in all Germanic languages, the exponents of [D] (GOTH *-m*, RUN *-mr*, ON *-m(r)*, OE *-m* etc.) probably continue the plural (post-)PIE [I] ending *-mĩs*, possibly also the plural (post-)PIE [D] ending *-mus* (cf. Old Lithuanian *-mus*, Old Church Slavonic *-mъ*),

f. OHG and OS singular [I] of the *a*-stems (OHG *-u*, OS *-u*) points unambiguously to the inherited singular PIE [I] *-oh*$_1$.

In addition, I assume that there is no reason to view [AB] as a distinct living member of the case system of PG. There are, of course, traces of [AB]

[6] Only the facts regarding the *a*- and *ō*-stems are given in the text; other paradigms are omitted for the sake of clarity.

[7] Old Saxon displays two endings here: *-a*/*-e* and *-u*. The variation *-a* ~ *-e* is connected with certain problems of OS orthography. See, for example, Boutkan (1995: 152).

[8] The exact reconstruction of this form is problematic and to some extent theoretical. The ending meant is the one (possibly) found in Vedic Sanskrit *-ā* and Lithuanian *-à*.

forms in Germanic (Bammesberger 1990: 12, Boutkan 1995: 181), but there are no signs whatsoever of its continuing to be a full-fledged grammatical case. Therefore, I consider [AB] to have been lost still in the PG period.

## 3. The Old English evidence

Generally speaking, the OE declensional system is similar to the ones attested in other Germanic languages and can be traced back to the declensional system of PG without serious difficulties. There is, however, at least one form that should attract our attention. It is the [I] of the *a*-stems in the singular: EOE *-i* (in later OE > *-e*, which makes it indiscernible from the singular [D] EOE *-æ* > OE *-e*).

As can easily be noticed, this morphological form diverges from the [I] of the *a*-stems attested in the singular in the remaining WG languages. The [I] attested in the singular in OHG and OS is *-u*. This ending, and possibly GOTH *-a* as well, is undoubtedly old; as mentioned above, it is believed to continue the PIE singular [I] *-oh₁*. Therefore, another explanation must be sought for the OE ending. Although a number of solutions have been proposed, in my opinion the form has not gained the attention it desires.

According to Hirt (1932: 36), Dahl (1938: 46), Krahe (1942: 10), Campbell (1959: 223), Sievers-Brunner (1965: 195) and Bammesberger (1990: 43), the OE forms in *-i* must represent the PIE singular [L] in *-ei̯*. This idea is credited to Eduard Sievers (1882) and although it is dismissed by Guxman *et al.* (1963: 142), it may be regarded as the standard explanation.[9] The hypothesis involves the semantic shift [L] > [I] in the singular; however, it must be born in mind that the EOE *-i* forms sometimes display locative meanings, which could be considered archaic, e.g. *on bergi* 'on the hill,' found in the Thornhill Cross inscription (Dahl 1938: 47), and *þys geri* 'this year' (Bammesberger 1990: 43).[10] As no better solution has been proposed, it appears that this one must be accepted. [11]

## 4. Implications and conclusions

What do the above-mentioned facts mean for the reconstruction of PG and the membership of its case system? The basic question that must be answered is whether the evidence from the oldest Germanic languages enables us to con-

---

[9] Curiously, neither Boutkan (1995) nor Ringe (2006) mention EOE [I] *-i*.

[10] The latter is a less clear example of a temporal locative.

[11] Importantly, the hypothesis also implies that EOE singular [D] *-æ* is derived from PIE *-o-ei̯*, i.e., the 'real' singular PIE [D]. Otherwise, the assumed developments would have had to be extremely complicated and improbable.

sider [L] as a separate case in PG.[12] While it is, obviously, hardly possible to give a confident answer, I would suggest the following: the independent, paradigmatic singular OE [I] ending *-i* is the strongest piece of evidence pointing to the potential independent status of [L] in the case system of PG. Nevertheless, the evidence is by no means clinching. It is not impossible to imagine a situation in which the PIE singular [I] and [L] would have merged already in PG, the *a*-stems retaining the forms *-ō* < PIE *-oh*$_1$ and *-ī* < PIE *-ei̯* with no difference in meaning; later, some dialects would have generalized *-ō* (OHG, OS), and others *-ī* (OE).[13] The only indication pointing towards a possible semantic difference between *-ō* and *-ī* in PG is that the EOE [I] singular ending *-i* appears to be used in a locative function at times, which suggests that it might represent the PG [L] singular, while the OHG, OS *-u* would go back to a separate PG category, the [I] singular *-ō*.

The above considerations are, of course, to a large extent hypothetical. Proving that [L] existed as a separate case in the inflectional system of PG seems hardly possible with the evidence available today. Therefore, the question in the title must remain unanswered: PG could have had a case system comprising [N], [G], [D], [AC], [I], [L], and [V], but it could also have had a case system comprising only [N], [G], [D], [AC], [I], and [V]. Nevertheless, the point worth stressing is that it is Old English, and not the most archaic Germanic dialects such as Runic or Gothic, that offers the most valuable material here.[14] It is puzzling why the authors of two recent authoritative studies on PG, Boutkan (1995), and Ringe (2006), do not deal with these forms.

## References


Arumaa, P. (1985). *Urslavische Grammatik.* Band III. *Formenlehre.* Heidelberg: Carl Winter.

Bammesberger, A. (1984). *A Sketch of Diachronic English Morphology.* Regensburg: Friedrich Pustet.

Bammesberger, A. (1990). *Die Morphologie des urgermanischen Nomens.* Heidelberg: Carl Winter.

Boutkan, D. (1995). *The Germanic 'Auslautgesetze'.* Amsterdam/Atlanta: Rodopi.

Braune-Reiffenstein, W. (2004). *Althochdeutsche Grammatik* I. 15. *Auflage bearbeitet von Ingo Reiffenstein.* Tübingen: Max Niemeyer.


[12] The various Germanic adverbial forms which possibly represent fossilized locatives are of no interest here; the problem concerns the status of [L] as a distinct value of an inflectional category of the language.

[13] No part of the evidence seems to exclude this possibility, on the condition that we assume the singular [D] forms of WG to represent old datives and not locatives.

[14] Also interesting and perhaps relevant are the so-called 'endingless datives' occurring in OHG, OS and OE. However, their history is very obscure and cannot be dealt with here; suffice it to say that some scholars consider such forms to represent old locatives as well (Boutkan 1995: 382, Braune-Reiffenstein 2004: 185, Campbell 1959: 224, Sievers-Brunner 1965: 196).

Campbell, A. (1959). *Old English Grammar*. Oxford: Oxford University Press.

Clackson, J. (2007). *Indo-European Linguistics*. Cambridge: Cambridge University Press.

Dahl, I. (1938). *Substantival Inflexion in Early Old English. Vocalic Stems*. Lund: Gleerup.

Fortson, B. (2004). *Indo-European Language and Culture*. Malden: Blackwell.

Guxman, M. M. *et al.* (1963). *Sravniteľnaja grammatika germanskix jazykov.* Tom III. *Morfologija.* Moscow: Izdateľstvo Akademii Nauk SSSR.

Hirt, H. (1932). *Handbuch des Urgermanischen.* Teil II. *Stammbildungs- und Flexionslehre*. Heidelberg: Carl Winter.

Krahe, H. (1942). *Germanische Sprachwissenschaft.* Teil II. *Formenlehre.* Berlin: de Gruyter.

Must, G. (1953). The genitive singular of *o*-stems in Germanic. *Language* 29: 301–303.

Prokosch, E. (1939). *A Comparative Germanic Grammar*. Philadelphia: University of Pennsylvania Press.

Ringe, D. (2006). *A Linguistic History of English*. Vol. I. *From Proto-Indo-European to Proto-Germanic*. New York: Oxford University Press.

Sievers, E. (1882). Der angelsächsische instrumental. *Beiträge zur Geschichte der Deutschen Sprache und Literatur* 8: 325–333.

Sievers-Brunner, K. (1965). *Altenglische Grammatik. Nach der Angelsächsischen Grammatik von Eduard Sievers*. Tübingen: Max Niemeyer.

Tichy, E. (2004). *Indogermanistisches Grundwissen*. Berlin: Hempen.

*Marta Ruda*
Jagiellonian University, Kraków

# TWO SYNTACTIC SYSTEMS IN ONE MIND: THE INFLUENCE OF PROCESSING L2 GRAMMAR ON SYNTACTIC PROCESSING IN L1*

## 1. Introduction

Knowledge of more than one language has only recently been recognized as a factor which influences the use of the native language. 'Reverse' or 'backward' transfer, as it is sometimes termed, is described by Cook (2003) as having either positive, negative or neutral effects on native language production and comprehension. Categorizing an example of the phenomenon in question along the lines of this distinction may, however, be susceptible to criticism, since it seems to depend on subjective justification. The focus of the present paper is to present some of the recent findings concerning the influence of the second language (L2) on the use and perception of syntactic structures in the first language (L1). I will concentrate here on the views on priming and the problem of language attrition and try to show that similarities and differences between the syntax of two languages, e.g. Polish and English, could prove an interesting area for future research.

## 2. Linguistic interference

It has not been more than a decade since the influence of L2 on L1 began to arouse linguists' interest. Although in one of the most influential books on language contact, Weinreich (1970) did not exclude the possibility for either language of the bilingual to be influenced by the other, at first mainly the ef-

* For helpful comments and suggestions, I would like to thank Zofia Wodniecka-Chlipalska and Ewa Willim. Thanks also to Sławomir Zdziebko for stimulating discussions and encouragement.

fects of L1 on L2 were investigated. As the influence of L2 on L1 is hard to detect unless L1 has undergone erosion and become markedly different from the norm, it usually cannot be studied without employing sophisticated experimental methods and equipment. However, with the development of research into interlanguage the study of the nature of mutual relations between the languages in the speaker's mind has started to be approached from different angles and identifying the areas of the influence of L2 on L1 has become the subject of numerous studies. One of the recent studies which aimed at testing the hypothesis that extensive exposure to L2 influences L1 was conducted by Mikhaylova (2006) among late Russian-English bilinguals. Among the bilinguals who were at equal levels of proficiency in L2 and who were equally exposed to it, the linguistic intuitions in L1 were found to be affected in a similar way. Although the study demonstrated that L2 influence on native-speaker intuitions is more noticeable on the lexico-semantic than on the morphosyntactic level, it does not diminish the importance of conducting research in the domain of the grammatical aspects of interlanguage.

### 2.1. Parsing

Considerable amount of attention has recently been devoted to the study of parsing strategies or, in other words, the processes used to assign words in a sentence to syntactic categories. Parsing assigns hierarchical structure to linear strings of sounds and is thus indispensable in the process of comprehending speech. Bilinguals are exposed to different types of biases when living in bilingual communities and a growing body of research supports the hypothesis that parsing processes in L1 may be affected due to exposure to L2. For example, Dussias (2001, 2004) and Dussias and Sagarra (2007) used the eye tracking method to examine the preferences of relative clause attachment in the linguistic context of complex noun phrases (N1-of-N2-RC) similar to the structure shown in (1) below:

(1) She was in love with the son of the linguist who lives in Kraków.

The experiment reported in Dussias (2001, 2004) and Dussias and Sagarra (2007) was based on the differences in relative clause attachment preferences between two groups of speakers of English and Spanish. The group of speakers of English as their L1 and Spanish as their L2 tended to attach a relative clause to the syntactically lower noun, whereas the group of speakers of Spanish as their L1 and English as their L2 attached it to the syntactically higher noun. This means that an English speaker reading (1) is most likely to understand that it is the linguist and not his son who lives in Kraków. For the speakers speaking Spanish as their L1 presented with the translation of the sentence (which has a similar structure to the English one as far as the noun phrases are concerned), the relative clause is attached to the higher noun *son*. What the results of the research showed was that the Spanish-English bilinguals who had been extensively exposed to English were likely to process the sentences in Spanish using the strategies characteristic of their L2 (English). This suggests that in proficient bilinguals who are immersed in an L2 environment, parsing strategies employed in L2 comprehension become more available to the processor and are used regardless of the language of the input. A plausible implication is that parsing decisions depend on frequency-based exposure and that there is a competition between alternative structures in the speaker's mind, which are understood as pieces of linguistic information stored in memory. The degree and speed of activation of alternative structures are determined by the frequency of particular successful resolutions.

### 2.2. Priming

Research methods based on speakers' tendency to rely on similar syntactic structures in the production and interpretation of utterances are a tool with the help of which psycholinguists try to gain insight into the mechanisms governing human speech. It has been experimentally shown that speakers tend to use structures which they have recently produced or heard, even if different structures would cover roughly the same meaning (Loebel and Bock 2003, Schoonbaert *et al.* 2005, Bernolet *et al.* 2007). In psychology, this type of mental processes is referred to as priming, i.e., a process of increasing the availability of some information in an individual's mind by exposure to stimuli which activate the information. For example, the speaker may be more likely to use a passive construction after first hearing or producing a passive sentence.

#### 2.2.1. Priming in L1

Priming has become a powerful tool for investigating the representation of syntactic structures in the mind of the speaker and the observations that it occurs in languages other than English and in different types of constructions, in production and comprehension as well as in isolation and dialogue, have been supported by experimental evidence. For example, eye-movement experiments with special focus on language comprehension were conducted by Carminati *et al.* (2008), who used double-object dative and prepositional dative constructions. The purpose of the study was to evaluate whether priming during comprehension is due to the anticipation of a particular structure or is rather caused by specific animacy features of the first postverbal noun. Due to the fact that changes in the animacy of the nouns occurring in prime constructions had no effect on priming, it seems that it is the abstract structural features rather than lexico-semantic features that are primed.

An extensive review of the research on priming was provided by Pickering and Ferreira (2008), who argued, among other things, that the phenomenon of structural priming may be taken as a piece of evidence for autonomous (in contrast to lexically-based) syntactic representations. According to them, sentences containing the locative *by*-phrase served as primes for passives with the agentive *by*-phrase and further, in the production of prepositional or double-object dative sentences, the effect of priming was not altered by the mismatches of the prime and the target in terms of postverbal argument modification (e.g. presence or absence of a relative clause). They explained these facts using a phrase structure rule account, e.g., priming is observed when the rule VP → V NP PP is repeated to construct the target sentence, which may be illustrated with the following examples:

(2) VP → V NP PP
a. showed the picture to his mother;
b. showed the picture which he painted to his mother.

Both phrases illustrated in (2) can be described as being based on the same general phrase structure rule, which suggests that they may be constructed by implementing similar mental operations (with additional operations attaching the relative clause in the case of the second phrase). Pickering and Ferreira (2008) suggested further that the results of the research on priming in comprehension and from production to comprehension imply that the two processes utilize the same, or at least closely connected, syntactic representations. As can be seen from the presented facts, priming can prove to be a very fruitful method in research on different aspects of linguistic knowledge and it can be expected to play a greater role in future psycholinguistic research on the relations between L1 and L2 in the human mind.

### 2.2.2. Cross-linguistic priming

There have also been experiments investigating whether a structure in one language may serve as a prime for a structure in another language. In one such study, Loebel and Bock (2003) used English and German dative structures and English and German passives. That prepositional dative and double-object dative constructions are congruent in English and German is shown in (3) and (4) below:

(3) Prepositional dative:
a. The girl bought a newspaper for the blind woman.
b. Das Mädchen kaufte eine Zeitung für die blinde Frau.

(4) Double-object dative:
a. The girl bought the blind woman a newspaper.
b. Das Mädchen kaufte der blinden Frau eine Zeitung.

However, the situation with the passive is different due to the fact that in the German equivalent of a passive English sentence, the passive participle is in the sentence-final position:

(5) Passive:
a. The concert was *attended* by many people.
b. Das Konzert wurde von vielen Leuten *besucht*.

Loebel and Bock's (2003) study showed that while active datives primed one another, passive constructions did not. According to the authors, this may be due to the discrepancies in the structure of the latter constructions in the two languages. Similar experiments have been conducted with the use of different structures in English and German as well as in English and other languages, including Spanish and Dutch. Whenever the structures were identical, the effect of priming was observed. If the constructions differed, for example in word order, there was no effect of priming (cf. Bernolet *et al.* 2007).

The above findings confirm that there is a kind of interaction between the strategies used by the parser to process syntactic constructions in the two languages of bilingual speakers. Those and similar studies have led to the formulation of a hypothesis concerning the way in which syntactic information is stored in the bilingual's memory. It has been proposed that instead of being stored separately, at least some pieces of syntactic information concerning each of the languages may be shared between the languages. What follows from the research on cross-linguistic priming is that procedurally similar structures may be employed in producing similar grammatical constructions in both languages of the bilingual. This is treated as a piece of evidence in favor of the shared storage of syntax in the memory of the bilingual. In short, when the two languages of the bilingual have identical syntactic structures, the representations of the constructions are thought to be stored in memory as a single integrated piece of information.

## 3. Language attrition

In most general terms, language attrition may be referred to as the loss of a language or at least some parts of a language. In some studies, the nature of language attrition has been investigated in connection with the phenomenon of inhibition. Discussing the implications of the studies on the pathological states of the brain, Lenneberg (1967) pointed out that aphasic patients do not loose their language completely and that their inability to use language may rather be due to inhibitory factors such as anomalies influencing the activation or processing of speech. This accords with the facts presented in Fabbro (1999), who described two subjects living in the United States, who ceased using their L1 Finnish and L1 Japanese in early childhood. As adults, they reported having lost the ability to communicate in their native languages. However, when in the state of hypnosis, they spoke their mother tongues fluently when the age regression had been suggested by the experimenters. The results imply that the altered state of consciousness was conducive to overcoming the activation threshold which had become higher due to some inhibitory effects.

The focus of the majority of the latest experimental research on language attrition is on vocabulary, since lexical competence is the domain in which the degradation of L1 is most apparent. Levy *et al.* (2007) suggested that in addition to the disuse of the native language, a major factor leading to attrition is the extensive use of L2 phonological labels, which is connected with the need to inhibit L1. The results of two experiments conducted by Levy *et al.* (2007) showed that semantics, conversely to phonology, does not show the effect of inhibition. Since L1 labels for frequently-used concepts are exposed to inhibition more often than the less frequent concepts, the vocabulary items which pertain to the more frequent concepts are likely to be most vulnerable to the process of attrition.

The problem of endangered languages was introduced by Polinsky (1996) in her study of the variety of Russian spoken by Russian immigrants in the United States, which is referred to as American Russian. In her work, Polinsky proposed the comparison of a full language with a variety of the same language spoken in an environment where it is not the dominant language as a method of studying language disappearance. She defined attrition as an incomplete language competence, which may be the result of the loss of L1, its incomplete acquisition, pidginization, or other factors. Furthermore, she pointed out that acceptability judgments, which are an established method in studying full languages, are not reliable when conducting research in the domain of reduced languages. The claim was supported with fragments of interviews with American Russian speakers who exhibit a considerable tolerance for ungrammatical forms and lack confidence when asked to provide grammaticality judgments. This shows how important neuroimaging methods may become for the development of the field, since the results of experimental studies conducted with these methods are least subject to be influenced by the subjects' conscious thinking during experimental tasks. According to Polinsky (1996), speakers of American Russian have passive knowledge of their L1 vocabulary items, but lack direct access to them, which may be caused by infrequent use. This is consistent with the view that the speed of activation of particular pieces of information depends on the previous activation of the information. What is more, Polinsky showed that the structural interference of English is strongest in tasks involving direct translation from English, which is in line with the research on cross-linguistic priming discussed above.

Among the attrition phenomena investigated in Polinsky (1996) which may be directly related to the influence of English (L2) on Russian (L1) in American Russian speakers, is the tendency to replace Full Russian reflexive verbs with a combination of a transitive verb and an object as in (6):

(6) She combed her hair.

Based on her studies, Polinsky (1996) drew the conclusion that due to the positive correlation between lexical and structural loss, the vocabulary elicitation technique may serve as a reliable method of assessment of linguistic competence. However, it could be fruitful to investigate whether the type of structural information which is correlated with the lexical loss could be perceived as autonomous, or whether it is rather that the correlation holds between the loss of the lexical items and the structural information which has to be encoded in the lexicon.

What is also of importance to the present paper is the distinction between externally and internally induced language changes. The former are taken to be due to the influence of another language, whereas the latter are seen as a result of universal principles or the properties of the grammar of an attriting language. The second type of changes is the main subject of a paper by Pereltsvaig (forthcoming), who implements the Minimalist framework to interpret the data gathered by Polinsky.

The main point in Pereltsvaig's (forthcoming) article is that reduced grammars of languages such as American Russian lack uninterpretable features, roughly speaking, grammatical features which have no semantic import on the interpretation of the elements on which they are found, such as case on nouns and number and person on verbs. Interestingly, Radford (1997) provides a similar explanation for the simplification of morphology in Creole languages, which he illustrates with the English-based Jamaican Creole. He also points to the question of learnability, since it has been observed in the literature that uninterpretable features seem to be mastered by children with greater difficulty than interpretable features. These observations may serve as a starting point for the comparison of the status and distribution of interpretable and uninterpretable features in adult languages undergoing impoverishment on the one hand, and developing child languages on the other hand. Obviously, the

## 5. Conclusion

As has been shown, the effects of the use of L2 grammar on syntactic processing in L1 may be investigated using different methods. The results can serve as a starting point in searching for answers to various theoretical inquires. If differences between bilinguals and monolinguals were uncovered with, for example, the method proposed here for studying Polish-English bilinguals, this finding would be evidence in support of the hypothesis that L2 processing has a bearing on syntactic processing in L1. Such evidence could contribute to our understanding of the nature of syntactic knowledge of two languages in one mind and inform theories of language. In conclusion, the reactions of the human brain in linguistic situations could be conducive to developing linguistic theories pertaining to the mechanisms of the mind that are concerned with language.

## References

Abutalebi, J., Cappa, S. F., Perani, D. (2005). What can functional neuroimaging tell us about the bilingual brain? In: J. Kroll and A. de Groot (eds.). *Handbook of Bilingualism: Psycholinguistic Approaches.* Oxford: Oxford University Press. 497–515.

Bernolet, S., Hartsuiker, R., Pickering, M. (2007). Shared syntactic representations in bilinguals: evidence for the role of word-order repetition. *Journal of Experimental Psychology: Learning, Memory, and Cognition* 33: 931–949.

Carminati, M. N., van Gompel, R. P. G., Scheepers, Ch., Arai, M. (2008). Syntactic priming in comprehension: the role of argument order and animacy. *Journal of Experimental Psychology: Learning, Memory, and Cognition* 34: 1098–1110.

Cook, V. (2003). Changing the first language in the L2 user's mind. Draft 'Intro to L2 effects on the L1.' <http://www.homepage.ntlworld.com/vivian.c/SLA/Multicompetence/ EffectsIntro.htm>.

Dussias, P. E. (2001). Sentence parsing in fluent Spanish-English bilinguals. In: J. L. Nicol (ed.). *One Mind, Two Languages: Bilingual Language Processing.* Oxford: Blackwell. 159–176.

Dussias, P. E. (2004). Parsing a first language like a second: the erosion of L1 parsing strategies in Spanish-English bilinguals. *International Journal of Bilingualism* 3: 355–371.

Dussias, P. E., Sagarra, N. (2007). The effect of exposure on syntactic parsing in Spanish--English bilinguals. *Bilingualism: Language and Cognition* 10: 101–116.

Fabbro, F. (1999). *The Neurolinguistics of Bilingualism. An Introduction.* East Sussex: Psychology Press.

Frenck-Mestre, Ch. (2005). Ambiguities and anomalies: what can eye-movements and event-related potentials reveal about second language sentence processing? In: J. Kroll and A. de Groot (eds.). *Handbook of Bilingualism: Psycholinguistic Approaches.* Oxford: Oxford University Press. 268–285.

Hahne, A., Friederici, A. (2001). Processing a second language: late learners' comprehension mechanisms as revealed by event-related brain potentials. *Bilingualism: Language and Cognition* 4: 123–141.

Lenneberg, E. H. (1967). *Biological Foundations of Language.* New York: Wiley & Sons.

Levy, B. J., Mc Veigh, N. D., Marful, A., Anderson, M. C. (2007). Inhibiting your native language. The role of retrieval-induced forgetting during second-language acquisition. *Psychological Science* 18: 29–34.

Loebel, H., Bock, K. (2003). Structural priming across languages. *Linguistics* 41–5: 791–824.

Mikhaylova, A. (2006). L2 influence on L1 intuitions of Russian-English late bilinguals. <http://www.indiana.edu/~sls2006/Abstracts/ MikhaylovaSLS.doc>.

Pickering, M. J., Ferreira, V. S. (2008). Structural priming: a critical review. *Psychological Bulletin* 135: 427–459.

Pereltsvaig, A. (forthcoming). What does American Russian tell us about language? *Journal of Slavic Linguistics.*

Polinsky, M. (1996). *American Russian: An Endangered Language?* San Diego: University of California.

Radford, A. (1997). *Syntactic Theory and the Structure of English. A Minimalist Approach.* Cambridge: Cambridge University Press.

Schoonbaert, S., Hartsuiker, R. J., Pickering, M. J. (2005). Translation equivalence enhances cross-linguistic syntactic priming. Poster presented at the CUNY conference, Tucson, Arizona. <http://www.users.ugent.be/~rhartsui/ISB5/ SofieCuny.ppt>.

Weinreich, U. (1970). *Languages in Contact. Findings and Problems.* Paris: Mouton.

*Olga Trendak*
University of Łódź

# DEDUCTIVE OR INDUCTIVE? A BRIEF ANALYSIS OF TWO TYPES OF GRAMMAR INSTRUCTION

## 1. Introduction

The received view on language learning and teaching is based on the idea that the goal of language acquisition is communicative competence, which is commonly postulated to comprise four distinct types of knowledge and skills: linguistic, sociolinguistic, pragmatic, and strategic. Once perceived as the sole key to success with language, linguistic competence comprises knowledge of the grammar and vocabulary of a language and the ability to use words and syntactic structures effectively, i.e., accurately and meaningfully, in a spontaneous way.

At the same time, views on the role of grammar in the learning and teaching of a language vary greatly. For some, grammar is simply a set of rules to be presented and practised to ensure accuracy; for others, grammar need not even be taught, as learners will acquire it on their own on the basis of the language input that they are exposed to in the process of language acquisition. The former perspective owes much of its persistence to the popularity of the Grammar Translation Method. The latter is the more recent view often taken by the proponents of communicative and proficiency-based teaching.

Regardless of the orientation, the role of grammar instruction in learning and teaching a language cannot be denied. What is at stake is how to ensure the use of grammar that is accurate, meaningful and appropriate to the situation. Although most attention in teaching grammar is nowadays given to issues such as interface vs. non-interface position, focus on form vs. focus on forms, and efficient and corrective feedback (Ellis 2006), the question whether grammar should be learned and taught deductively or inductively is still a basic problem that teachers must resolve in their everyday professional life. The aim of this paper is to present a balanced view of the strengths as well as weaknesses of the two approaches to developing grammatical knowledge and to provide both specialists and beginners in the teaching profession with an up-to-date resource on current research in SLA regarding grammar instruction. The focus is on explicit knowledge, i.e. awareness of grammatical rules, which can be developed by means of deduction or induction. Explicit knowledge, together with implicit knowledge, which is knowledge of rules acquired unconsciously on the basis of exposure to linguistic data, are the two integral parts into which linguistic knowledge is divided, as shown in Fig. 1 below.

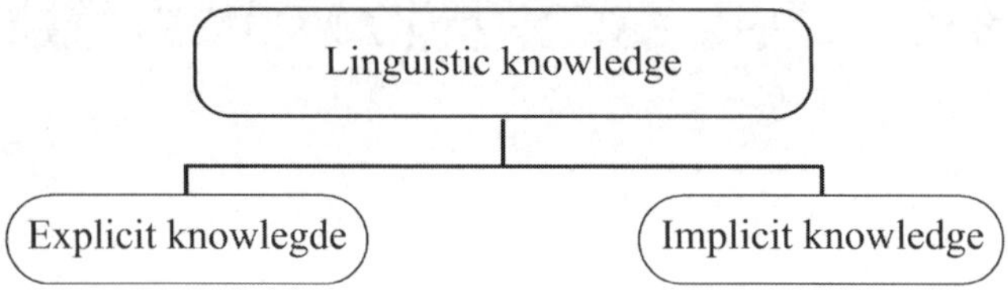


Fig. 1. The division of linguistic knowledge

## 2. Defining deductive instruction

Deductive instruction, also referred to as rule-driven learning, aims at introducing a new grammatical concept or structure overtly, that is by stating directly what a given rule is and when and how it should be applied in the target language. Learners are first presented with a rule and then asked to engage in activities that check the understanding of the target feature. Although its sequence is relatively fixed, deductive instruction allows for some variations, for example in terms of the degree of explicitness or intensity (Sharwood Smith 1981). The teacher may provide the learners with a full rule or simply give a part of it. The degree of elaboration, or in other words the time devoted to presenting a certain rule, may also vary (Sharwood Smith 1981). Eisenstein (1980) also mentions the source and manner of presentation. The former may be the teacher, the students, or a textbook. As for the latter, a given feature may be presented in a written way, orally, or as a mixture of both.

There are various ways in which a rule can be implemented. Pawlak (2006) suggests making use of demonstrations. For example, when discussing subject pronouns, the teacher can point to different students in the classroom. The teacher may also introduce charts (e.g. tables containing information about the English articles). Iconic devices and formulas can be widely applied. The former may take on the form of a scale. For example, modal verbs can be ranked on a scale to convey the difference in the degree of necessity or other modal notions that they encode. The latter may be useful when introducing new tenses (e.g. the constructions involving the auxiliary *has/have* + Past Participle). Finally, there are pictures which can be an interesting alternative to writing rules on the blackboard. For example, when introducing the Present Continuous Tense, the teacher may use a picture depicting people engaged in various activities. However, it needs to be borne in mind that on certain occasions teachers tend to make extensive use of explicit explanations to make certain that learners comprehend the rule. In a group of beginners, the teacher may fall back on L1. However, as many SLA specialists suggest, it would be a much better solution to resort to L1 only in situations when the learners have evident problems with rule comprehension. What should also be carefully considered is metalanguage and the level of abstractness (Pawlak 2006). Cross-linguistic comparison could also make the learners focus on the rule to a greater extent and, hopefully, arouse their interest.

Presenting a new grammatical material deductively may appear beneficial both to the learner and to the teacher. First of all, it is extremely time-saving. The teacher knows how much time he/she will devote to the explanation of a new item and, thus, can carefully plan his/her lesson. This is why deductive instruction ensures an orderly organization of lessons. It also equips learners with a mental map of the material (Johnson 2001, Thornbury 1999).

Furthermore, direct explicit instruction may be suitable for students who wish to learn a foreign language quickly. Having been presented with a certain rule directly, instead of having to formulate it on their own, students economize on time. This way of presenting a new item may be appreciated by students preparing for examinations such as FCE, CAE, DFB, or other language certificates. A course whose aim is to prepare students for an exam is usually very intensive and sometimes introducing a grammatical rule explicitly may be the best way to save time.

In addition, conducting a lesson in this manner can, to some extent, give the learners a feeling of safety, as they are aware of what they can expect during their classes. As deductive explicit instruction covers the introduced grammatical issues in a highly systematic way, it also contributes to the feeling of regularity and order among students. Moreover, according to Thornbury (1999: 30), deductive instruction "respects the intelligence and maturity of many – especially adult – students, and acknowledges the role of cognitive processes in language acquisition." This way of presenting new grammatical material may prove useful to students who are in favor of analytical learning and who do not wish to squander their time on working out a rule on their own. Lastly, deduction enables teachers to tackle certain points as they come up, without preparing for them beforehand (Thornbury 1999).

Nonetheless, deductive instruction has received severe criticism. First of all, it bears some resemblance to the Grammar Translation Method, as there is no or very little room left for communication (Pawlak 2006). What is more, in Thornbury's (1999) opinion, starting a lesson with grammar may discourage particularly younger and less advanced learners, who may lack the necessary terminology and may not be in a position to comprehend all the introduced concepts. Moreover, since learners do not have any influence on the way the material is presented, there is a risk that they will not internalize it. Furthermore, the opponents of deductive instruction claim that it focuses on the teacher rather than on the student. Teacher talking time takes up most of the classes; at the stage of rule introduction, students are only supposed to listen. Because it is the teacher who is mostly engaged in talking, there is little (if any) time for interaction or a communicative exchange of information. Conducting classes in this manner may promote a transmission-style form of learning (Pawlak 2006). It has also been suggested that learners may leave the classroom thinking that language learning revolves only around learning rules.

Finally, direct grammar instruction may simply seem mundane, especially to inquisitive younger learners and those who feel a need to explore the target language and make their own discoveries. This approach may be restrictive and may even discourage students from looking at a language holistically. As a result, instead of looking at many aspects of language at a time, students may focus just on a particular chunk, phrase or structure. Therefore, deductive grammar instruction may curb learners' autonomy. They may leave the classroom with a feeling that the most significant part of the lesson has been done for them and they have not contributed to the development of the class in any way.

## 3. Inductive teaching

According to Pawlak (2006: 270), in inductive instruction "learners are first exposed to instances of language use, they are expected to attend to a specific grammatical structure in the data, pinpoint recurrent patterns, and arrive at their own generalizations which account for the regularities perceived." Even though this type of instruction entails a shift from the specific to the general, Pawlak (2006) goes on to mention certain possible variations. Importantly, the input may be varied, for example learners may work on pictures, drawings, surveys, dialogues, unrelated sentences, etc. As far as the manner of data presentation is concerned, the material may be introduced orally, in writing, and sometimes in both media. In addition, learners' attention to the target feature may be drawn in a number of ways, for example by typographical alterations such as underlining, italics, bolding, intonational changes, or increased frequency. What is more, learners may be asked to perform different activities concerning the target structure, namely gap-filling, rule-completion, matching, or giving answers that demand the application of a given linguistic feature. Lastly, the degree of metalinguistic awareness may vary.

This manner of presenting new grammatical material has been widely praised. One reason is that as rules are discovered rather than presented explicitly, they are more likely to fit learners' mental structures and be easier to remember (Thornbury 1999). The teacher does not provide the learners with a rule or expect them to memorize it and use it when doing various exercises. Instead, the learners are the ones who figure out the rule. Having made a discovery on their own, learners are more likely to remember it for a longer time. Such a way of introducing grammar is more stimulating and engaging for the learners, who may feel that they have contributed to the lesson and, as a result, leave the classroom satisfied or even fulfilled. This, in turn, leads to another advantage of the inductive approach, namely fostering students' independence and autonomy (Pawlak 2006). Learners feel that, at least during some part of the class, they are in charge and can co-create the lesson and that they are needed because their presence and involvement in the lesson matter. By inducing the rules on their own, learners, or at least some of them, develop an interest in the language and the way it works. Making discoveries increases students' inquisitiveness.

Furthermore, inductive instruction enables learners to see how the target feature is used in communication and to recognize the form-meaning-function mappings prior to being acquainted with the rules (Brown 2001). Inductive teaching can be also very rewarding for the teacher. Seeing learners actively involved in the lesson and perceiving their interest motivates each teacher to work and makes them feel needed. In addition, if problem-solving activities are carried out collaboratively and in the target language, there is more time to practise the target form (Thornbury 1999).

However, inductive instruction has various drawbacks. To start with, it is extremely time- and energy-consuming. To conduct an interesting and involving lesson that will go according to his/her plan, the teacher has to devote a lot of time preparing it. Learners also need a certain amount of time to focus on the materials provided and to arrive at a rule. This time may be squandered if they hypothesize a wrong rule (Pawlak 2006). Worse yet, there is a possibility that learners might fail to work out a rule at all. Then, their willingness to learn decreases and so does the teacher's motivation, as he/she had devoted a great deal of time and energy to prepare what turned out to be an unsuccessful lesson. Resorting to explicit explanation seems inevitable in such a situation.

Inductive instruction might also be too big a challenge for those learners who prefer being provided with a rule instead of inferring it on their own. As observed by Pawlak (2006: 282–283), some learners "might see no point in getting engaged in lengthy inductive tasks and perceive them as an unnecessary waste of time that could be devoted to deploying the structures in communicative activities." There is also a risk that when engaged in performing the task, learners, particularly those less proficient ones, will resort to their L1. Lastly, there are grammatical phenomena, for example aspect and modality, that may be difficult for the teacher to present in an inductive manner, no matter how meticulously they plan their presentation (Thornbury 1999).

## 4. Conclusions

On the whole, it is fair to say that research aimed at comparing the effectiveness of the two types of instruction has not supported the superiority of the inductive approach (Pawlak 2006). Several studies did not reveal major differences between the two approaches (Abraham 1985, Shaffer 1989, Rosa and O'Neill 1999) and only one argued in favor of induction over deduction (Herron and Tomasello 1992). There were also several studies that proved deductive instruction to be the more efficacious one (Seliger 1987, Robinson 1996, Ellis 1993, DeKeyser 1995, Erlam 2003).

As discussed in this paper, opinions concerning the two approaches to grammar instruction are greatly divided. In current research, teachers are advised that "[s]imple rules may best be taught deductively" (Ellis 2006: 96) and that "(...) when a particular linguistic rule is rather convoluted, it may make more sense to present a grammar structure deductively" (Larsen-Freeman 2001: 264). Indirectly, such statements indicate that both deductive and inductive grammar instruction have a role to play in developing linguistic competence. The choice must be based on considering the benefits of one of the methods against the other in the context in which learning and teaching take place and it must be guided by the overall aim of developing the knowledge of how to use grammar in an accurate and meaningful way which is appropriate to the situation of language use.

## References

Abraham, R. (1985). Field independence-dependence and the teaching of grammar. *TESOL Quarterly* 20: 689–702.

Brown, H. D. (2001). *Teaching by Principles. An Interactive Approach to Language Pedagogy*. White Plains, NY: Pearson Education.

DeKeyser, R. (1995). Learning second language grammar rules: An experiment with a miniature linguistic system. *Studies in Second Language Acquisition* 17: 379–410.

Eisenstein, M. (1980). Grammatical explanations in ESL: teach the student, not the method. *TESOL Talk* 11: 3–13.

Ellis, N. (1993). Rules and instances in foreign language learning: interactions of explicit and implicit knowledge. *European Journal of Cognitive Psychology* 5: 289–318.

Ellis, R. (2006). Current issues in the teaching of grammar: an SLA perspective. *TESOL Quarterly* 40: 83–107

Erlam, R. (2003). The effects of deductive and inductive instruction on the acquisition of direct object pronouns in French as a second language. *Modern Language Journal* 87: 242–260.

Herron, C., Tomasello, M. (1992). Acquiring grammatical structures by guided instruction. *French Review* 65: 708–718.

Johnson, K. (2001). *An Introduction to Foreign Language Learning and Teaching*. Harlow: Pearson Education

Larsen-Freeman, D. (2001). Teaching grammar. In: M. Celce-Murcia (ed.). *Teaching English as a Second or Foreign Language.* Boston: Heinle & Heinle. 264–265.

Pawlak, M. (2006). *The Place of Form Focused Instruction in the Foreign Language Classroom.* Kalisz/Poznań: Wydawnictwo WPA UAM.

Robinson, P. (1996). Learning simple and complex second language rules under implicit, incidental, rule-search, and instructed conditions. *Studies in Second Language Acquisition* 18: 27–68.

Rosa, R., O'Neill, M. (1999). Explicitness, intake and the issue of awareness. *Studies in Second Language Acquisition* 21: 511–556.

Seliger, H. (1987). Inductive method and deductive method in language teaching: a reexamination. *International Review of Applied Linguists in Language Teaching* 13: 1–18.

Shaffer, C. (1989). A comparison of inductive and deductive approaches to teaching foreign languages. *Applied Linguistics* 73: 395–403.

Sharwood Smith, M. (1981). Consciousness-raising and the second language learner. *Applied Linguistics* 2: 159–168.

Thornbury, S. (1999). *How to Teach Grammar*. Harlow: Pearson Education.

*Radosław Turniak*
University of Łódź

# DOES INTERTEXTUALITY HAVE TO BE TEXTUAL?

## 1. Introduction

The aim of this paper is to discuss poetry-music intertextual devices mainly in relation to three music genres: blues, jazz, and pop. I focus here on some instances of form-based intertextuality in poetry, suggest several ways of tracing such intertexts, and discuss their significance as an object of analysis for literary criticism, translation studies as well as linguistics.

## 2. Form-based intertextuality

As Sumera (2002: 465) puts it, "the term 'intertextuality,' introduced by Julia Kristeva, is now generally used to express the view that practically all new texts refer to texts that have already been written." This very general definition will suit the purpose of this paper, but there is one important caveat. Namely, Sumera makes a direct link between texts and the written mode, suggesting that his work will revolve (only) around literary texts. Nevertheless, despite the common-sense association of texts with writing, since de Saussure's *Course in General Linguistics* the term 'text' has been applied to any entity produced by the languages of the cinema, painting, music, architecture, fashion, etc. According to Allen (2000: 174), these languages "involve production of complex patterns of encoding, re-encoding, allusion, echo, transposing of previous systems and codes."[1] As this paper analyses some instances of musical intertexts which appear in poetry, I will assume here a broad interpretation of 'text', which extends in its application outside written literary texts. My

[1] It is important to remember that the tradition of understanding 'text' broadly goes back to Jakobson (1956/1989).

aim is to trace intertexts which are connected with rhythm and the philosophy and conventions of a particular music genre, i.e., intertexts which are form-based. Such allusions are obviously 'intertextual', but they are not intertextual in a sense which takes us back to specific lyrics of a music 'text.'

## 3. First indications of possible intertexts

Authors themselves often provide some indications of upcoming music intertexts in the title of a poem. The indication might be a direct reference to a music genre, as is the case of W. H. Auden's *Lullaby*, Adrian Henri's *Adrian Henri's Talking After Christmas Blues* or Langston Hughes' *The Weary Blues*. Nevertheless, we cannot assume that mere inclusion of a music term in the title means that a particular genre is going to be reworked in a poem.

A perfect example is Philip Larkin's *Aubade*. Although the poem alludes to the 18th century French song evoking or accompanying daybreak, it proceeds to reconstructing the patterns of blues, as observed by Leggett (1999). It should be noticed that there is a tangible connection between the mood of the aubade and blues, and the latter might be considered as stemming from the former. However, traditional lovers tormented by the prospect of parting are absent in Larkin's *Aubade*, and the poem's structure follows directly the arrangement of a blues composition. The title of the poem suggests the disposition of the speaking persona, which is clearly blues-like, yet readers might be mistaken when it comes to foreshadowing the form and the contents of the poem.

The indication in the title may also take the form of an indirect reference, as in Larkin's *For Sidney Bechet* or Hughes' *Ma Rainey*. Both titles allude to a musician and a specific music genre that is performed by each of them: correspondingly, jazz and blues.

Nevertheless, such prominent suggestions are sometimes omitted by specialists working on a particular piece of text, who fail to acknowledge the importance of the first piece of intertextual information that might be extracted from the poem. For example, Feliks Woroszylski's translation of *Adrian Henri's Talking After Christmas Blues* completely disregards the blues intertextuality of the poem and fails to transfer any intertextual effects present in the original, whether rhythmical or philosophical. As a result, the poem has lost one of its most distinguishing features in Woroszylski's translation.

## 4. Floating lines as an intertextual device

Another prominent intertextual device is the use of so-called floating lines. As defined in Oliver (1968: 68), a floating line is "a single line or even a phrase, that will move from one blues to another, will be given new rhymes and meaning and will be juxtaposed with new ideas." A floating line cannot be linked with a particular music text, as it is part of the convention and appears in variations in many works belonging to a particular music genre. An example of a floating line might be the exclamation "yeah, yeah, yeah" in rock music, "play that thing" in jazz, and the opening statement "woke up this morning" or "I work all day" in blues. All of them appear in a plethora of songs.

The inclusion of floating lines in poetry provides scholars with a further context in which to analyze the text. Identifying such a line is often vital for a successful analysis. Thus, "Well, I woke up this mornin' it was Christmas Day," the opening line of *Adrian Henri's Talking After Christmas Blues*, should prompt a translation that will keep the rhythm and conventions of blues, particularly the idea of 'going down' and lack of rhymes in particular places. In a similar vein, the opening lines of *Aubade*:

(1) I work all day, and get half drunk at night.
Waking at four to soundless dark, I stare

should immediately suggest the blues convention to a literary critic and guide him or her to an analysis of the poem not in terms of panic-stricken moaning, but as an almost cathartic experience (Leggett 1999: 112).

## 5. Structure as an intertextual device

Music intertextuality may also be achieved by reworking or alluding to the song structure inherent to a specific music genre. An example is *Annus Mirabilis* by Larkin and its structure, itself an intertext leading to rock and roll music, a term "sometimes used broadly to refer to the popular music of the second half of the $20^{th}$ century" (Bradley 1992: 87). The poem is the only instance in Larkin's poetry where the first stanza is repeated at the end of the poem with some slight modification to indicate the sense of closure and to strengthen the poem's connection to popular music:

(2) Sexual intercourse began
In nineteen sixty-three
(which was rather late for me) –
Between the end of the Chatterley ban
And the Beatles' first LP.
(...)
So life was never better than
In nineteen sixty-three
(Though just too late for me) –

Between the end of the Chatterley ban
And the Beatles' first LP.

This pattern dominated the pop music of the fifties and the sixties of 20th century and it appears in numerous songs by Buddy Holly, The Who, early works of The Beatles and many others. As Leggett (1999: 190) observes, "the 'pop music' feeling readers may pick up from the poem is thus easily accounted for; its overall structure and sense of closure are effects we associate with music rather than poetry."

The classic blues stanza and song structure is also quite stable. The form "crystallized in the first decade of the 20th century as a three-line stanza in which the second line repeated the first, thus enabling the blues singer to improvise a third, rhyming line while singing the second" (Oliver 1968: 13). An intertext to such structure is present, for example, in Sterling A. Brown's poem *Riverbank Blues*, which starts in the following way:

(3) A man git his feet set in a sticky mudbank,
A man git dis yellow water in his blood,
No need for hopin', no need for doin' (...).

Although the first two lines are not identical, the repetition of the first four syllables and the observed syntactic parallelism, juxtaposed vividly with the third line, leads the reader directly to the convention of blues.

## 6. Meter as an intertextual device

The most important way to create an intertext to music in poetry is by the use of a certain meter to produce a rhythm that resembles or imitates rhythmical conventions of a particular music genre. While it is possible to say that every good poem follows some kind of a 'musical' pattern, the comparison offered here will focus on some specific techniques that intertextual poems share with the music genre that is the basis for intertexts.

The first feature to be discussed is syncopation. According to *The New Grove Dictionary of Jazz,* it is "the regular shifting of each beat in a measured pattern by the same amount ahead of or behind its normal position in that pattern" (Kernfeld 1988: 203). It is used in many music genres, but it is especially prominent in blues and jazz. Analyzing the meter of the last five lines of the poem *For Sidney Bechet*:

(4) (...)
On me your voice falls as they say love should,
Like an enormous yes. My Crescent City
Is where your speech alone is understood,

And greeted as the natural noise of good,
Scattering long-haired grief and scored pity.

William Harmon notices "the finely syncopated rhythm in the last line – trochee, iamb, spondee, iamb, trochee – where the scazon [the substitution of a trochee for the concluding iamb] delivers the final rhyme a syllable sooner than our ear expects" (quoted in Leggett 1999: 73). This particular use of meter serves as an another intertext in the poem and without acknowledging this fact the last line is ambiguous and hardly understandable.

Syncopation can also be noticed in the opening lines of *Aubade*, quoted in section 4 above. As Leggett (1999: 96) points out, "the basic rhythm of the line is iambic, but its two spondees shift the accents on all and half a syllable sooner than the iambic pattern calls for." While it is not a syncopation in a strict sense, the tension between the words and the rhythmical pattern is clearly present. According to Riffaterre (1979/1988), in intertextual poems there are certain obscure places and anomalies in the rhythm when the lines are incongruous to the context, drawing the reader's attention and signaling the presence of an intertext (cf. also Leggett 1999: 95). The poetic equivalent of syncopation in the first line of *Aubade* calls for an explanation, which can be offered only if the rhythm of blues is taken into consideration. Other attempts at syncopation might be spotted in Adrian Henri's *Adrian Henri's Talking After Christmas Blues* and Langston Hughes' *The Weary Blues*. The latter foreshadows the upcoming rhythm distortion in the first line: "Droning a drowsy syncopated tune."

Rock music follows a completely different pattern. Robert Leszczyński, an acclaimed critic of popular music, repeated throughout numerous interviews that a perfect rock song should resemble Led Zeppelin's *Stairway to Heaven* in the sense that it should start slowly, then build up the tension and accelerate in "meter" to end with the return to the tempo of the beginning of the song. Many masterpieces use this rhythmical pattern, to mention *A Day in the Life* by The Beatles or *One* by Metallica. It is also visible, or rather heard, in the poem *Trumny z Ikei* by Bohdan Zadura. The first stanza is slow, reflective and the meter does not stand out as intertextual:

(5) Ford transit gloria mundi ale z fordem K to nie przejdzie
A na transita już za późno i na tej pysznej
Reklamie nie zarobimy pieniędzy by kupić to autko,
najlepiej karminowe, jak zabawka.

However, after the eighth stanza the pace of the poem accelerates, which is achieved by alliteration and enumeration, for example:

(6) i głupiejesz od tych firan i zazdrostek
kratek pasków poduszek poduszeczek przytulanek
kołder pokrowców szaf szafek i szafeczek
kubków kubeczków czajniczków...

To complete the design, the last stanza shifts back to the unhurried, contemplative pace, thus fulfilling all the requirements of a perfect rock song.

Larkin's *Annus Mirabilis* is an example of pop rhythm taking control over the 'lyrics' of the poem. The first thing that strikes readers as unusual is the strange choice of words, including 'sexual intercourse,' 'LP' and the use of parenthesis. However, when the poem is read, the phrases fit naturally into the rhythm and they follow the poem's melody. As Leggett (1999: 191) notices, "in the popular music the interest is normally not in the words themselves but in the 'interplay and intimacy between words, voice and music,' and this is the effect the stanza of *Annus Mirabilis* achieves." Even the intrusion of parenthesis, which breaks the rhythm, should be treated as a music intertext. It is reminiscent of the background vocal of many pop songs, when the 'lead' lyrics are accompanied by short phrases sung by one of the band members, usually to make a personal remark or fill in the space unoccupied by lyrics with additional information. On the whole, the structure of the poem, the rhythm and intertexts make *Annus Mirabilis* a perfect example of the music-poetry intertextuality at work, as observed by Ricks (1982: 8), for whom it is "a poem to be sung rather than simply read."

## 7. Practical implications of music intertexts

Tracing any of the above-mentioned instances of intertextuality can be crucial when it comes to a proper analysis of a poem. For a linguist, it might be a means of disambiguating lines, which seem obscure without the knowledge of the intertext. The phrase *scored pity* from the poem *For Sidney Bechet* may be interpreted in various ways, as the adjective *scored* might denote winning points in a game, berating, grading, keeping a record, acquiring points in a game, or even gaining a sexual success. However, only when treated as an intertext and not an allusion is the significance of the phrase narrowed down to taking down notes to be later performed. Therefore, *scored pity* signifies the opposition between jazz, which is improvised and produced immediately without playing from the notes, and the old-fashioned types of music, which heavily relied on notes, lacking the authenticity and spontaneity of jazz. For a translator, such music intertexts should be guidelines for the proper rendition of a poem, for example highlighting the necessary rhymes and phrases which cannot be omitted in translation. With the knowledge of extra-linguistic intertexts, the lines from Adrian Henri's *Adrian Henri's Talking After Christmas Blues* included in the influential anthology entitled *The Mersey Sound*:

(7) there was
mincepies
brandy
nuts and raisins
...mashedpotato
but no you

which follow a very specific "stairwell" pattern and tellingly omit the rhyme in the final stanza, would have never been rendered into Polish as trite:

(8) Pasztet koniak orzechy wszystko pachniało wabiło
– ale ciebie nie było.

For a literary critic approaching a poem as intertextual, this experience might produce new interpretations, sometimes important and influential, as is Leggett's advance on *Aubade*. If the poem is approached with the blues convention in mind, the apparent panic and the 'whining' mood of the poem turns out to be a conventional, realistic blues approach to death, far from snivelling and tragedy, but an almost cathartic experience, an affirmation of life and everyday chores. Therefore, scholars should pay greater attention to intertexts, which are not obvious and apparent at first glance. Discovering a connection between literature and music might be highly profitable, whatever the interest of the scholar might be.

## 8. Conclusions

While discussing music-poetry intertexts, it is important to bear in mind that intertexts do not always have to refer to the lyrics of a particular music 'text' and that intertextuality does not always have to be textual in the narrow sense of a 'linguistic text.' Hence, scholars analyzing a poem which is suspected of employing intertextual devices connected with music should research a particular music convention rather than limit themselves to searching for obvious textual allusions. Paying greater attention to less apparent, yet equally important intertextual devices, such as the use of floating lines and structural or metrical intertexts, should be of primary importance when working with such a poem.

## Sources

Auden, W. H. (1999). *Collected Poems*. London: Faber and Faber.
Brown, A. S. (1980). *The Collected Poems of Sterling A. Brown*. New York: HarperCollins.
Henri, A. (1972). *Adrian Henri's Talking After Christmas Blues*. Translated by Feliks Woroszylski. *Literatura na Świecie* 2: 33–34.
Henri, A., McGough, R., Patten, B. (1973). *The Mersey Sound*. London: Penguin.
Larkin, P. (2003) *Collected Poems*. London: The Marvell Press and Faber.
Rampersad, A. (1994). *The Collected Poems of Langston Hughes*. New York: Vintage Classics.
Zadura, B. (2005). *Wiersze zebrane. Tom 2*. Wrocław: Biuro Literackie.

## References

Allen, G. (2000). *Intertextuality*. London: Routledge.
Bradley, D. (1992). *Understanding Rock 'n' Roll: Popular Music in Britain 1955–1964*. Buckingham: Open University Press.
Jakobson, R. (1956/1989). Dwa aspekty języka i dwa typy zakłóceń afatycznych (Two aspects of language and two types of aphasic disturbances). In: M. R. Mayenowa (ed.). *W poszukiwaniu istoty języka 1. Wybór pism*. Warszawa: PIW. 150–175.
Kernefeld, B. (ed.). (1988). *The New Grove Dictionary of Jazz*. New York: St. Martin's Press.
Leggett, B. J. (1999). *Larkin's Blues*. Baton Rouge: Louisiana State University Press.
Oliver, P. (1968). *Aspects of the Blues Tradition*. New York: Oak Publications.
Ricks, C. (1982). Like something almost being said. In: A. Thwaite (ed.). *Larkin at Sixty*. London: The Marvell Press.
Riffaterre, M. (1979/1988). Semiotyka intertekstualna: interpretant. *Pamiętnik Literacki* 79(1): 297–314.
Sumera, A. (2002). Intertextuality in literary translation. In: B. Lewandowska and M. Thelen (eds.). *Translation and Meaning. Part 6*. Maastricht: Universitaire Pers. 465–469.

*Jakub Wosik*
University of Łódź

# ON NOTE-TAKING IN CONSECUTIVE INTERPRETING

## 1. Introduction

Today, it would probably be difficult to imagine any international meeting without interpreters. Interpreters work in different situations, environments and organizations. They are employed by companies, courts, the police, health services, public administration, international organisations. From the point of view of the many environments in which interpreters work, different types of interpreting can be distinguished: court interpreting (courts of law), community interpreting (police, health service, public administration), conference interpreting (international organizations, conferences, meetings), to mention some common varieties of interpreting. The separate type of interpreting that I want to concentrate upon in this paper is consecutive interpreting (CI). In section 2, a brief history of conference interpreting, which embraces CI, will be presented by way of providing some background for later discussion. The aim of section 3 is to define interpreting and to distinguish between its main kinds. In section 4, I address in some detail several aspects of interpreting that make up for the individuality of consecutive interpreting and present the views on the theoretical aspects of note-taking during CI. This section also includes a discussion of the results of a questionnaire that I have given to ca. 30 interpreters, both beginner and experienced, to find out whether the suggestions that CI theorists make concerning note-taking are implemented in the practice of CI. Section 5 concludes the discussion.

## 2. A short history of CI

Conference interpreting emerged as a separate and a highly esteemed discipline around the turn of the 19$^{th}$ century. Some specialists in the theory of translation and interpreting suggest that conference interpreting started in 1878 during the Congress of Berlin, others suggest that its origins can be traced back to the Paris Peace Conference in 1898. The most widely accepted proposal was made by Herbert (1978: 5), according to whom "conference interpreting only actually started during the First World War." From that moment on, interpreting has become an indispensable part of international life. Interpreters had their role to play during the historical meetings of the League of Nations and the War Crimes Trials of the International Military Tribunal in Nuremberg (Delisle and Woodsworth 1995: 250). Today, there is no international organization that does not employ interpreters; the European Parliament itself "employs approximately 350 staff interpreters and has at its disposal a reserve of some 2,500 freelance interpreters (auxiliary conference interpreters) whom it calls on very regularly as required to cover its needs."[1] Needless to say, the European Parliament is just one of many bodies of the European Union, not to mention other international organizations such as the United Nations or NATO.

## 3. What is interpreting?

To define consecutive interpreting, one must first refer to the general definition of interpreting. Probably the shortest definition of interpreting is due to Jones (2002: 3), who defines it as "immediate oral translation." According to *The New Shorter Oxford English Dictionary*, an interpreter is "a person, especially an official, who translates orally the words of people speaking different languages" (Brown 1993). However, what needs to be added is that like translators of written texts, interpreters are not merely facilitators of communication between parties that do not share a common language. They are mediators between two or more parties "bridging the cultural and conceptual gaps separating the participants during a meeting" (Jones 2002: 4). For a good interpreter, it is not enough to have a proficient command of both (or more) languages that the participants are using. An interpreter must understand both the explicit meaning communicated by the speakers and the implicit meanings that they convey, (s)he must be able to grasp a metaphor, a joke, etc. and even more importantly, (s)he must be able to mediate this to the other participant(s).

The definitions presented above are simple, general definitions of a broad notion of interpreting. However, as mentioned above, there is no one type of interpreting. There could not be only one variety of interpreting, as different situations and environments require different types of interpreting. The number of the different modes of interpreting varies, depending on the source and the method of classification that is adopted. The division of interpreting that is most popular and widely agreed upon in linguistics is into simultaneous and consecutive interpreting.

1 http://www.europarl.europa.eu.

According to Kopczyński (1980: 12), during simultaneous interpreting (SI) "the message is interpreted while it is being spoken," whereas during CI "the message is first spoken and then interpreted." Tryuk (2007) enriches the description of the consecutive mode by adding that during CI interpreting takes place after listening to the whole text or only a part of it. Moreover, when the interpreter conducts CI, (s)he may compose notes using a special way of notation, on the basis of which (s)he reproduces the text in the target language (Tryuk 2007: 50).

It seems that also the description of SI calls for a small addition: it is true that during SI interpreting takes place at the same time the original speech is being delivered; however, before the interpreter may start rendering the source text into the target text, (s)he has to wait a few seconds. The reason for this lag is the need to wait for the first idea mentioned by the speaker to be complete. The length of the lag depends on the source language, e.g. it is considerably longer, reaching even as much as ten seconds when the source language is German, the reason being that German main verbs often appear at the end of a sentence (for example when the sentence contains a modal verb), and the sentences themselves tend to be rather lengthy.

The division of interpreting into SI and CI is only a general one. These two modes are further divided into several types of interpreting, depending on a variety of factors taken into consideration. For the needs of this article, let us choose two distinguishing aspects: the way of interpreting, and the environment in which interpreting is conducted.

As far as the former is concerned, SI can be divided into: "live interpreting (the so-called a vista interpreting), whispered interpreting, simultaneous proper (with the use of special equipment)" (Kopczyński and Markiewicz 1997: 291–297). As for the latter factor, the environment in which interpreting takes place, SI falls into conference interpreting (during conferences and meetings), liaison interpreting (when an interpreter accompanies a person; also called escort interpreting or chuchotage), legal interpreting (interpreting in courts), community interpreting (for immigrants at police stations, hospitals, etc.), telephone interpreting, sign language interpreting, etc.

## 4. Consecutive interpreting

This section is concerned with the issue central to the paper: the description of CI. Jones (2002: 12–42) presents a coherent model of the processes involved in CI, which he divides into three stages: understanding, analyzing and re-expression. Let us first concentrate on the understanding part.

The most important question the interpreter has to be asking himself or herself during the whole speech of a given speaker is: "What does the speaker mean?" However obvious this may sound, it is not as obvious as it may seem at first sight. The interpreter needs to be asking himself or herself this question continuously to identify the ideas conveyed by the speaker and grasp the intended message over and above the meanings that are communicated by the words that the speaker utters.

Almost immediately after the first stage (or even during it) begins the second stage: analysis. During this stage, the interpreter moves on to analyzing the ideas that (s)he has identified and is to re-express. According to Jones (2002: 25–26), what the recipients of a speech need to find out is "who? what? when? Or more specifically: who does what, and when, and who says or thinks what." This forms a basis for the analysis of the main ideas of the message to be expressed. It is also essential to conduct an analysis of the linguistic style of the speech. In order to re-express the source text well, the interpreter must decide what type of speech (s)he is listening to and, therefore, what language style (s)he needs to adopt for re-expression. Another important aspect of analysis are sentence- and text-connectives. As Jones (2002: 31) argues, "[a] speech is not just a sequence of juxtaposed sentences." A speech is a logical argument, where one idea is (or at least should be) connected with the preceding idea or ideas as well as with the idea(s) to come.

After the main ideas have been identified, the language style and the connectives analyzed, the time has come for re-expression of the speech. The interpreter often has to speak to a gathering of people. That is why (s)he has to have a clear, strong voice, has to speak at a steady sustained pace without unnecessary pauses, obviously cannot have any speech problems (e.g. stammering), and has to be able to speak the target language well. One other aspect of crucial importance to the process of consecutive interpreting, an aspect included in almost all descriptions of CI by presented theoreticians of interpreting, is note-taking during CI.

### 4.1. The rationale for note-taking during CI

There are different approaches to note-taking and their role in CI. Specialists such as Rozan (2004) and Seleskovitch (1978) (representing the French school of interpreting) advocate a minimalist or a limited method of taking notes during CI, whereby the interpreter uses only a small number of symbols and abbreviations relying more on his or her memory and using the notes just as waypoints for speech rendition in the target language. Others, like Matyssek (1989), who represents the approach still advocated in the German school of interpreting, take an opposite stand and stress the need for a sophisticated system of symbols and abbreviations, converting almost everything which is understood and analyzed into an almost hieroglyphic text (after Tryuk 2007). In view of the latter approach, it would be a rather bold claim to say that notes are not as essential as one might think and yet, as Jones (2002: 43) observes, "[t]he essential part of a consecutive interpreter's work is done in the activities already described: understanding, analysis, re-expression. If these are not done correctly, the best notes in the world will not make you a good interpreter."

Could note-taking be independent of the circumstances in which CI takes place? Obviously, if the interpreter is to translate single short messages of the speaker, (s)he can easily render the ST without using notes. On the other hand, in a situation in which (s)he has to interpret larger chunks of speech, possibly extended in time, note-taking becomes a helpful instrument for several reasons.

First, it enables the interpreter to relieve his or her memory, who can take down the main ideas and any other information which is sometimes difficult or impossible to memorize using even the most efficient mnemonic techniques. Furthermore, taking notes of the main ideas enables active listening. The interpreter does not have to spend his or her effort on remembering and instead, (s)he can jot the points to remember down and continue listening, understanding, and analyzing. Finally, well-made notes reflect the outline of the speech. One of the important abilities of a consecutive interpreter is to learn not only to take down the ideas and connectives, but also to record the structure of the speech: the length of certain segments and the pauses dividing individual ideas.

### 4.2. The art of note-taking for CI: theoretical aspects

The reader of this article is more likely than not to have listened to a university lecture and made some notes, perhaps a fair amount of them. Does this mean that anyone having some experience in taking notes during a lecture has the note-taking skills required for CI? Unfortunately for the person, perhaps, and fortunately for the profession, the answer is negative. This is because taking notes during a lecture has very little in common with taking notes during consecutive interpreting, which every beginner consecutive interpreter painfully learns at the beginning of his or her training.

The reason for the discrepancy between the two modes of taking notes stems from the length of the life of notes. While notes made by a student should stay meaningful for a fairly long time, for example at least one semester, notes produced during CI will be of no use when the meeting or the conference is over. Often, notes taken during CI are destroyed by the interpreter at the request of the contracting parties as part of the confidentiality policy of the contract. When taking notes during a lecture, students need to create a faithful record of the speech, paying attention to every detail. Such a record would be of no use to an interpreter, mainly because it would take him or her too much time to sift through the notes while re-expressing the speech. Therefore, the interpreter's notes must be more of a skeleton outline of the speech, and less of a record.

What, then, should be taken down during CI? If not full sentences, not even separate clauses, then what should an interpreter note? Theoreticians argue that, as the notes are to constitute a kind of a skeleton of the speech, they should have the most important elements of the speech: its main ideas. However, having only the main ideas would not be enough, as ideas come in a speech in a logical sequence, either as developments of previously mentioned ideas or to introduce contrast. This is why it is important to note the links between the main ideas. This aspect of language should not be underestimated. "An idea can be distorted completely if its relation to the previous idea is not clearly indicated" (Rozan 1956/2004: 18). Since notes are supposed to relieve memory, interpreters are advised to note down figures, dates, proper names, etc. There is no need for trying to remember several place names, countries, rivers, etc., if they can be jotted down, relieving the interpreter's memory for understanding and analysis. Note-taking is vital especially in the case of lists.

When it comes to the form which the notes taken during CI should have, one of the most famous and often quoted page layouts is the 'diagonal layout' proposed by Rozan in his book *La prise de notes dans l'interpretation consecutive* (1956). The diagonal layout is a page structuring where the interpreter notes main ideas of the speech diagonally from upper left to lower right. Jones (2002: 49) also refers to this layout, incorporating in it his 'subject-verb-object analysis.' He proposes that all key-words belonging to the subject group of a main idea should appear on the upper left, key verbs should appear somewhat central, and the key-words related to the object should appear on the lower right.

In addition, theoreticians studying CI stress that it is best to write on a 15 by 20 centimeter stenographer's note-pad. It is easy to write on, easy to carry and the pages may be turned with no trouble at all. Turning the pages is very important as it may be best to note only on the recto side of a sheet of paper. This way the unnecessary turning of the pad is omitted. And there may be a lot of page turning, since sometimes it may be better to note only one idea on one page for the sake of clarity and meaningfulness.

According to specialists, using any of the modern pens is useless and often only complicates the whole process. The best choice is the old and faithful lead pencil. One should also remember that in order to take advantage of the notes, they must be legible. Therefore, it is advisable to write in capital letters or at least write letters of a considerable size.

### 4.3. Note-taking in CI: from theory to practice

To find out whether the theoretical guidelines for note-taking during CI are implemented by practicing interpreters in their daily professional activity, I have asked a group of ca. 30 English-Polish interpreters about their practice of consecutive interpreting. The group consisted of both beginner interpreters studying the art of interpreting, and professional interpreters with at least 10-year-long experience in the profession. The study revealed several interesting regularities.

As mentioned above, note-taking during CI is not necessary, but it is very helpful for the proper rendition of the source utterance. The questionnaire revealed that an overwhelming majority of both beginner and experienced interpreters do make or use notes during CI. Only one interpreter from the entire group admitted to almost never composing or using notes during CI. Among those who do take notes during interpreting a rather predictable tendency could be observed: beginner interpreters depended more on their notes when rendering the original utterance than experienced interpreters.

Recall that while CI theorists stress the importance of taking down the mains ideas to be re-expressed as well as the devices that link the ideas logically, note-taking is highly recommended in the case of interpreting lists, figures, dates, names, etc. Indeed, all the subjects in the questionnaire adhered to the above-mentioned rules in their CI practice.

The biggest discrepancy between theory and practice is related to the organization of the notes taken during CI. Less than 25% of the professional interpreters who filled out the questionnaire in question admitted to arranging their notes according to a defined page layout. In the case of the beginner interpreters that I have investigated, the percentage falls below 15%.

In the introduction to the 2004 translation of Rozan's *La prise de notes dans l'interpretation consecutive*, one can read a witty division of consecutive interpreters. Among the various types (for example, "the dyed in the wood 'remember-it-all' colleagues (...), »noters-of-words«") Rozan (1956/2004: 9) proposes "the 'symbol-for-everything' interpreters." There has always been the question of what to abbreviate or where to use a symbol and instead of what. As even Rozan notices, there are professionals who tend to have a symbol for everything. However, in my study, only 35% of the professionals admit to using special systems of symbols and abbreviations (compared with over 40% of beginner consecutive interpreters).

As for the technical aspects of note-taking at CI, none of the beginner interpreters from the group reported using a stenographer's notepad and only one reported using a pencil instead of a pen or ball-pen. All the other beginner interpreters write on loose pages or in notebooks and usually with a pen. The ratio is slightly better in the case of professionals: about 15% use a stenographer's notepad and all others use notebooks or loose pages. As for writing equipment, none of the professional interpreters reported using a pencil; the majority have reported using a pen.

## 5. Conclusion

The results of the informal questionnaire administered to a group of ca. 30 beginner and professional consecutive interpreters discussed in this paper reveals considerable lack of convergence between the theory and practice of CI. Although the group was perhaps too small to draw firm conclusions, it nevertheless indicates a certain regularity. Namely, what it highlights is that the issue of note-taking during CI is a fairly personal activity, which is developed by each interpreter individually. It seems, then, that any system of note-taking advocated by theorists of CI should be considered more as guidelines how to compose notes than a fixed frame which should be learnt by heart and implemented as quickly as possible. On the basis of the results of the small survey discussed here, one could not agree more with Rozan when he states that the system that he himself advocates "is not to be followed blindly. It should be the inspiration; it should be adapted according to whatever best suits each individual" (Rozan 1956/2004: 11).

## References

Brown, L. (ed.). (1993). *The New Shorter Oxford English Dictionary*. Oxford: Oxford University Press.

Delisle, J., Woodsworth, J. (1995). *Translators through History*. Amsterdam: John Benjamins Publishing Company.

Jones, R. (2002). *Conference Interpreting Explained*. Manchester: St. Jerome Publishing Ltd.

Herbert, J. (1978). How conference interpretation grew. In: D. Gerver and W. Sinaiko (eds.). *Language, Interpretation and Communication*. New York and London: Plenus Press. 5–9.

Kopczyński, A. (1980). *Conference Interpreting*. Poznań: Wydawnictwo Naukowe Uniwersytetu im. Adama Mickiewicza.

Kopczyński, A., Markiewicz, A. (1997). Conference text types in Poland and the teaching of interpretation. In: E. Fleischmann (ed.). *Translationsdidaktik. Grundfrangen der Übersetzungswissenschaft*. Tübingen: G. Narr Verlag. 291–297.

Rozan, J.-F. (1956/2004). *Note-taking in Consecutive Interpreting*. Kraków: Tertium.

Seleskovitch, D. (1978). *Interpreting for International Conferences*. Washington D.C.: Pen and Booth.

Tryuk, M. (2007). *Przekład ustny konferencyjny*. Warszawa: Wydawnictwo Naukowe PWN.

*Sławomir Zdziebko*
Jagiellonian University, Kraków

# A USERS' GUIDE TO CVCV PHONOLOGY*

## 1. Introduction

The late 1980s and early 1990s brought a substantial shift in the views on the role of structures and derivations in phonology. The 1985 and 1990 papers by Kaye, Lowenstamm and Vergnaud postulated a static view that underlined the role of the lexicon and the structural relations between the segments of phonological representations. The aim of this paper is to present the main tenets of the continuation of the approach proposed in the above-mentioned works: CVCV Phonology presented in Scheer (1998, 2004). The paper is structured as follows: section 2 is devoted to the introduction of the syllabic constituent structure in CVCV. Section 3 is a presentation of the Empty Category Principle (ECP), which constitutes the very essence of the approach in question. The aim of section 4 is to present a brief typology of phonological processes within CVCV, with emphasis on their motivation. Section 5 gives a short summary of the facts presented in this paper.

## 2. Constituent structure

Syllabic constituent structure in CVCV consists of a string of onsets and nuclei following each other monotonously. The idea was first presented in Lowenstamm (1996) and has since influenced the works of many phonologists (cf., among others, Scheer 1998, 2004, Rowicka 1999, Szigetvári 1999, Cyran 2003).

* This paper is meant to make the reader familiar with the very basic concepts and mechanisms of CVCV Phonology, as presented in Scheer (2004). For different versions of CVCV see, for example, Rowicka (1999), Szigetvári (1999), and Cyran (2003). Since, obviously, it is not possible to introduce all of the said mechanisms, this work is aimed at providing enough background for an introductory reader to be able to follow more advanced articles in the theory. The background knowledge required to get full advantage of the information given in this work embraces some aspects of Autosegmental Phonology (Goldsmith 1990) and Generative Phonology in general (Kenstowicz and Kisseberth 1979).

Basic structural configurations like complex onsets, coda-onset clusters, short and long vowels, geminates and diphthongs are shown in (1):

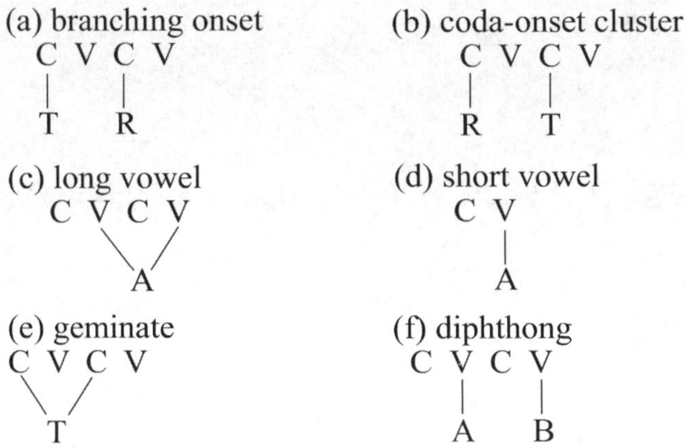


where:
T – any obstruent
R – any sonorant
A/B – any vowel

As far as examples are considered, the configurations in (1a) and (1b) can be found in the initial and final clusters of the English word /trend/, respectively. Configurations (1c) and (1d) can be illustrated with the Italian /faato/ 'fate.' A geminate is present, for example, in Moroccan Arabic /htrrts/ 's/he breaks,' and a diphthong in English /skai/. All those examples are graphically depicted under (2) below:

(2) Examples of structural configurations in CVCV:

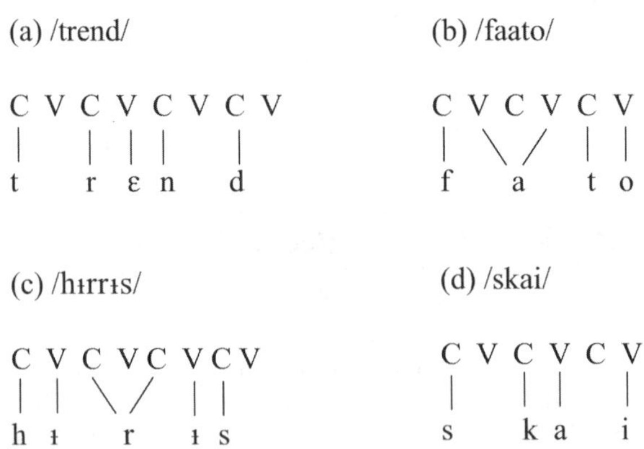

The main focus of the model are the phonotactic restrictions present in the phonological structure of the string and, to be more precise, the principles and parameters that govern the restrictions in questions. These principles and parameters manipulate two lateral relations whose source are vocalic positions: Government and Licensing. The former restricts the internal composition and/or organizations of a segment, the latter supports it.

The direction of both is, crucially, regressive. The effects of the lateral relations are most strikingly present in vowel-zero alternations, which lie at the very heart of CVCV, and the theory of lenition and fortition presented in Ségéral and Scheer (2001) and summarized in Scheer (2004). In particular, a vowel affected by Government may remain silent and its melodic material is not attached to the V position. Such a vowel loses its lateral potential, while a consonantal position that precedes it is not licensed and is prone to lenition. The effect of Government is also observed in the intervocalic position where the C position affected by the following V is also frequently weakened. On the other hand, consonants that follow governed vowels are affected only by licensing, which makes them strong. The role of the two lateral relations for the well-formedness of the phonological structure will be addressed in more detail later on in the paper (cf. section 3).

As the reader might have already noticed, the consonantal clusters in CVCV obligatorily enclose nuclei that are not melodically present on the surface. These empty nuclei constitute a characteristic feature of CVCV. They have been argued for by, among others, Kaye, Lowenstamm and Vergnaud (1990), Lowenstamm (1996, 1999), Gussmann and Harris (1998), Cyran (2003), and Scheer (2004). The arguments in support of empty nuclei in particular and empty categories in general in phonology are both theoretical and empirical in nature.

Firstly, both empty onsets and empty nuclei are a direct and inevitable consequence of the basic tenets of Autosegmental Phonology (Goldsmith 1990): empty C positions, empty V positions as well as floating melodic units must be generated automatically if the levels of melody and constituent structure are to be perceived as true autosegments. Secondly, the existence of empty nuclei and the fact that they are deprived of a lateral potential that their filled congeners have predicts a number of empirically correct effects. Among them are, for example, closed syllable shortening/laxing in Italian (Scheer 1998) and consonant weakening (/l/-vocalization) in Brazilian Portuguese (Scheer 2004) as well as the exact shape of syllables in many languages (the obligatory presence of vowels before clusters of falling sonority for example in English).

However, empty nuclei must be controlled. As has been underlined many times in the literature (cf., among others, Harris 1994: 191), the generative power of a representation that utilizes empty nuclei is enormous. Without any means to curtail it, any string of consonants enclosing empty nuclei is predicted to occur. As there are restrictions on the possible number of consonants in a string in all languages, CVCV needs a mechanism to account for the existence of such restrictions. This mechanism has been inherited, with a number of modifications, from the ancestor of CVCV, i.e. Government Phonology (GP) (Kaye, Lowenstamm and Vergnaud 1990, Charette 1991, Gussmann and Kaye 1993, Harris 1994, Gussmann 2007), and it is known as the Empty Category Principle (ECP). This principle is discussed in some detail in the next section.

## 3. Handling Empty Categories in CVCV

There are three mechanisms in CVCV that allow a nucleus to remain silent so that it does not surface phonetically nor is deleted from the representation along with the C position that it licenses. These mechanisms are presented in (3):

(3) Empty Category Principle (adopted from Scheer 2004):
A nucleus remains phonetically unexpressed iff it is:
(a) subject to Internuclear Government from the following nucleus, or
(b) subject to parametrical government when domain-final, or
(c) enclosed within a domain of Infrasegmental Government.

Internuclear Government refers to a relation that a filled nucleus (governor) contracts with a preceding nucleus (governee) to the effect that the latter remains silent. It is responsible, for example, for the existence of vowel-zero alternations in Polish words like *matka* 'mother$_{SG.NOM}$' – *matek* 'mother$_{PL.GEN}$'. The representations of *matka – matek* are provided in (4):

(4) Polish vowel-zero alternations:

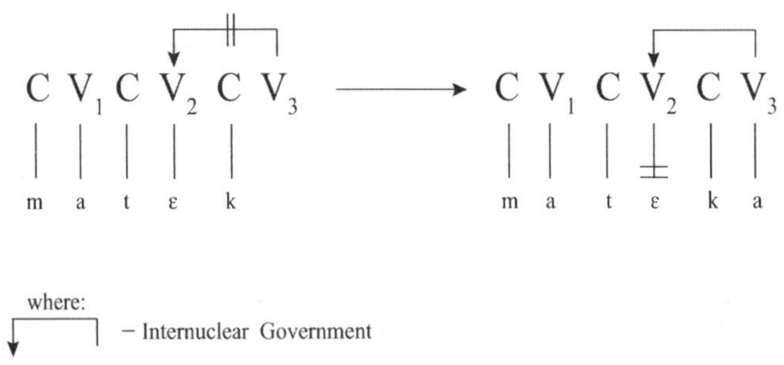

In (4a), the word /matɛk/ ends in an empty nucleus that is deprived of the governing potential. Not being subject to ECP, the empty category $V_2$ is pronounced. When an inflectional ending /a/ of nominative singular is added to the stem, the relation of Internuclear Government is contracted between $V_3$ and $V_2$ in (4b) to the effect that $V_2$ remains silent, which is indicated with the crossed association line.

The silencing of a domain-final nucleus is another development that CVCV inherited from GP.[1] In GP (and, by extension, in CVCV), it is assumed that every phonological domain ends in a nucleus. The idea of the existence of nuclei at the end of words has a theoretical basis. In GP (and later in many versions of CVCV), it is assumed that in order to exist, each and every onset must be licensed by a nucleus. However, in certain forms this nucleus is not expressed. Whether the final V position is pronounced is parametrically regulated:

(5) Final Empty Nucleus (FEN) parameter:
Govern the final empty nucleus: [OFF]/ON

(5) is said to work to the effect that there are systems where all domains surface as ending in vowels, such as Italian or Maori, and there are languages where words end either in vowels or in consonants, such as English or Hebrew. Once a novelty, nowadays the idea of empty categories in phonology is fairly established and for the theories like CVCV, it is a null hypothesis.

The third means that CVCV utilizes to ensure that empty categories remain unexpressed is Infrasegmental Government (IG). IG is a relation that takes place optionally (it may but does not have to take place when its conditions are fulfilled) at the level of melodic structure. It is licensed by a nuclear position that follows the second member of the IG domain. It is always headed by a sonorant due to a particular melodic make-up of this type of segments. Being subject to a relation established at the level of phonological primes, empty categories that are subject to IG seem to be invisible to certain phonological processes taking place at the level of skeleton and above it. For example, in Polish forms like /mondra/ 'clever$_{\text{F.SG.NOM}}$', where /d/ and /r/ participate in an IG relation, the empty nucleus is invisible to Internuclear Government, the source of which is the final V position.[2] For the sake of clarity, let us provide the representation for /mondra/:[3]

[1] For a detailed discussion and the impressive body of empirical evidence supporting the existence of final empty nuclei see Kaye (1990), Harris (1994), and Gussmann and Harris (1998).

[2] Another process for which nuclei enclosed within IG domains are invisible is stress assignment (Scheer 2004: 597-623).

[3] Only necessary structural relations are included in (6).

(6) Representation for Polish /mondra/:

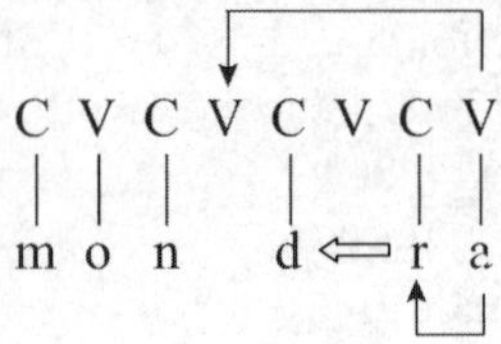


where:

– (Internuclear) Government

– Government Licensing (GL)

– Infrasegmental Government

In /mondra/ in (6), /d/ is governed by /r/, licensed to be head of the infrasegmental relation by the following V position. The nucleus enclosed within the IG domain is not pronounced. Crucially, it is also invisible to Government, which is directed at the preceding nucleus and allows it to exist and to remain silent.

To sum up, CVCV employs three mechanisms for the empty V positions to remain silent: Internuclear Government, FEN parameter and Infrasegmental Government. The first of them is an asymmetrical internuclear relation. It is head-final (left-directional) and its head is required to be phonetically expressed. The government that targets final nuclei is parametrically regulated. Therefore, final nuclei are either allowed to remain silent or obliged to surface phonetically. Finally, IG is another head-final relation, this time between consonants. It ensures that a nucleus is not only unexpressed but also invisible to Government. To exist, by virtue of IG it must be licensed by a following, expressed nucleus (Scheer 1998 and 2004). Now let us move on to a brief introduction of the possible processes within CVCV.

## 4. Phonological processes in CVCV: HIGH vs. LOW causality

In CVCV, there are two distinct areas of causality that may trigger phonological processes: HIGH and LOW. The processes triggered by the first one are traditionally referred to as syllabically-driven processes. The LOW(ER) processes can be characterized as triggered by and taking place at the level of melody. The HIGH (or UPPER) area is responsible for syllabic motivation for spreading (composition) or delinking (decomposition) of a given segment, the two operations available in CVCV that are of interest here. The forces available at the HIGH area have already been introduced as Licensing and Government. Some important characteristics of HIGH causality are: directionality (only regressive) and irrelevance of the melodic aspect of the source of a lateral relation (the trigger are V positions, not their quality). Although both government and licensing may have important consequences for the melodic make-up of their target, the exchange of primes between segments remains the function of the LOW(ER) part of the representation. Other important features of the LOW(ER) area are the adjacency of the trigger and the target and the fact that the melody-driven prime exchange may take place in both directions.

According to Scheer (2004), from which the above-mentioned criteria are adopted, a phonological process may be either exclusively HIGH or LOW in nature. An example of the former is /l/-vocalization in Brazilian Portuguese, where a liquid is deprived of melody and pronounced as a semivowel before a governed nucleus. This process is presented in (7):

(7) Examples of /l/-vocalization in Brazilian Portuguese:

| V_V | V_C | _# | |
|---|---|---|---|
| sa[ɫ]eiro | sa[w]gar | sa[w] | ‘salt cellar / to salt / salt’ |
| ca[ɫ]adu | ca[w]sa | ca[w] | ‘who is silent/trousers/lime’ |
| ma[ɫ]a | ma[w]vado | ma[w] | ‘suitcase, nasty, badly’ |
| mu[ɫ]a | sa[w]co | su[w] | ‘mule, furrow, South’ |
| vi[ɫ]a | fi[w]tro | vi[w] | ‘town, filter, mean’ |

In (7), the lateral deprived of Licensing (being followed by a governed nucleus) is weakened to [w]. The detailed examples of the process in question are shown in (8). The crossed line denotes lack of a given lateral force:

(8) /l/-vocalization in Brazilian Portuguese:

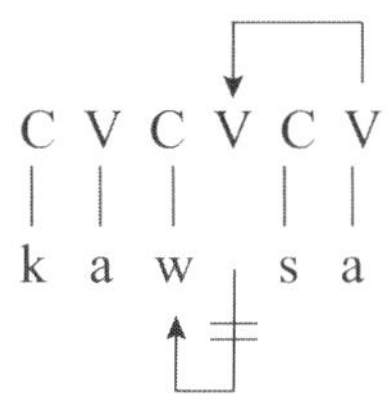


where:

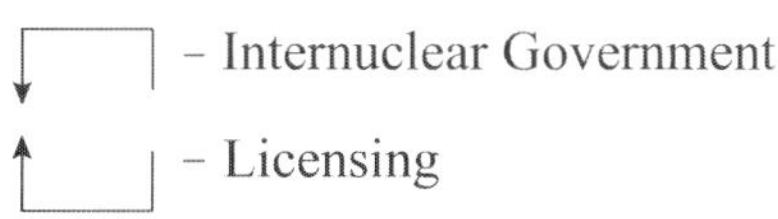

An example of a process triggered only by melody is vowel harmony in Turkish. Relevant data from Charette and Goksel (1998) are presented in (9):

(9) Vocalic harmony in Turkish:

| Stem | Gloss | Plural |
|---|---|---|
| kil | 'clay' | kil-ler |
| kʏl | 'ash' | kʏl-ler |
| kul | 'subject' | kul-lar |
| kel | 'bald patch' | kel-ler |
| kol | 'arm' | kol-lar |

In Turkish, all vowels within a domain must agree as to backness. Thus, the vowel alternant in the plural suffix depends on the quality of the vowel in the stem. This is analyzed as spreading of the [front] feature, which is represented in (10) as a monovalent prime:

(10) Vowel harmony in Turkish /keller/:

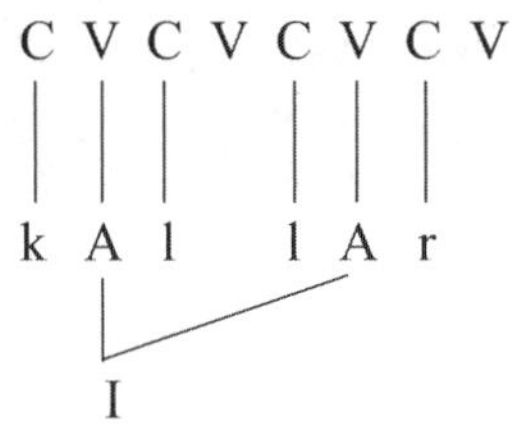


In (10), the monovalent prime that stands for frontness spreads right, on the prime that represents backness. The combination of the two primes is phonetically interpreted as /e/. What is important here is that the forces working in the UPPER area play no part in the process and, consequently, reference to them is avoided in the representation.

Both processes triggered by UPPER and LOWER causalities are subject to certain language-specific restrictions called Licensing Constraints. However, it is probably worth mentioning that the HIGHER processes are much more predictable, whereas the processes that take place at the level of melody are generally characterized by a high level of idiosyncrasy.

## 5. Summary

In this short paper, I have presented the basic tenets and theoretical machinery employed by CVCV phonology. To be more precise, I have introduced the concepts of syllabic constituent structure, Government and Licensing, the existence and motivations for Empty Nuclei and such aspects of ECP as Internuclear Government, the FEN parameter and Infrasegmental Government. Finally, I have given a taste of what phonological processes are possible in CVCV and I have classified them in accordance with their motivation. Readers interested in further discussion and functioning of CVCV are referred to studies listed in the References.

## References


Charette, M. (1991). *Conditions on Phonological Government.* Cambridge: Cambridge University Press.

Charette, M., Goksell, A. (1998). Licensing constraints and vowel harmony in Turkic languages. In: E. Cyran (ed.). *Structure and Interpretation.* Lublin: Folium. 65–88.

Cyran, E. (2003). *Complexity Scales and Licensing Strength in Phonology.* Lublin: Wydawnictwo KUL.

Goldsmith, J. (1990). *Autosegmental and Metrical Phonology.* Oxford: Blackwell.

Gussmann, E. (2007). *The Phonology of Polish.* Oxford: Oxford University Press.

Gussmann, E., Harris, J. (1998). Final codas: why the west was wrong. In: E. Cyran (ed.). *Structure and Interpretation.* Lublin: Folium. 139–162.

Gussmann, E., Kaye, J. (1993). Polish notes from a Dubrovnik cafe. *SOAS Working Papers in Linguistics and Phonetics* 3: 427–462.

Harris, J. (1994). *English Sound Structure.* Oxford: Blackwell.

Kaye, J. (1990). 'Coda' licensing. *Phonology Yearbook* 2: 305–328.

Kaye, J., Lowenstamm, J., Vergnaud J.-R. (1985). The internal structure of phonological representations: a theory of Charm and Government. *Phonology Yearbook* 2: 305–328.

Kaye, J., Lowenstamm, J., Vergnaud J.-R. (1990). Constituent structure and government in phonology. *Phonology Yearbook* 7: 193–231.

Kenstowicz, M., Kisseberth, C. (1979). *Generative Phonology. Description and Theory.* New York: Academic Press.

Lowenstamm, J. (1996). CV as the only syllable type. In: J. Durand and B. Laks (eds.). *Current Trends in Phonology. Models and Methods.* Manchester: ESRI. 419–441.

Lowenstamm, J. (1999). The beginning of the word. In: J. Rennison and K. Kühnhammer (eds.). *Phonologica 1996.* The Hague: Holland Academic Graphics. 153–166.

Rowicka, G. (1999). *On Ghost Vowels. A Strict CV Approach.* The Hague: Holland Academic Graphics.

Ségéral, P., Sheer, T. (2001). La Coda-Miroir. *Bulletin de la Société de Linguistique de Paris* 96. 107–152.

Scheer, T. (1998). Governing domains are head-final. In: E. Cyran (ed.). *Structure and Interpretation.* Lublin: Folium. 261–285.

Scheer, T. (2004). *A Lateral Theory of Phonology: What is CVCV, and Why Should It Be?* Berlin: Gruyter.

Szigetvári, P. (1999). *VC Phonology: a Theory of Consonant Lenition and Phonotactics.* Budapest: Eötvös Loránd University.

# ABOUT THE AUTHORS

**Paweł Błaszczyk** is a student at the Institute of English Philology, the Jagiellonian University of Kraków, and Head of the Linguistics Section of the Jagiellonian University Students' English Society. His main academic interests include literary and linguistic stylistics, cognitive aspects of translation, translation theory, and Ugro-Finnic languages, especially Finnish.

**Mikołaj Deckert** is affiliated with the Department of Translation Theory and Practice at the Institute of English Studies, the University of Łódź. His academic interests center on translation, pragmatics, language and cognition as well as media discourse.

**Dobromiła Jagiełła** is currently a Ph.D. student at the Faculty of Philology, the Jagiellonian University of Kraków. She is also a lecturer at the Foreign Languages Teacher Training College in Sucha Beskidzka. Her main academic interests include syntax, the syntax/semantics and pragmatics interface, and contrastive English-Polish linguistics.

**Marek Majer** is a student at the Institute of English Studies and the Institute of Southern Slavic Studies, the University of Łódź. He is mainly interested in diachronic comparative linguistics, especially Indo-European studies and the Slavic and Germanic languages.

**Marta Ruda** is a student at the Institute of English Philology and the Department of Hungarian Philology, the Jagiellonian University of Kraków. Her main fields of interest are: generative syntax, neurolinguistics, language acquisition, and psycholinguistic aspects of bilingualism.

**Olga Trendak** is a student at the Institute of English Studies, the University of Łódź. Her academic interests include second language acquisition, teaching methods, language learning strategies as well as focus on form and its impact on SLA.

**Radosław Turniak** is a student of the Institute of English Studies, the University of Łódź. His academic passions are: English poetry of the Sixties, its translation and translation criticism.

**Jakub Wosik**, a graduate of the Institute of English Studies, is currently a Ph.D. student at the Department of Pragmatics at the University of Łódź. He is a professional translator and interpreter in the Polish-English pair, specializing in legal and political discourse.

**Sławomir Zdziebko**, a student of the Institute of English Philology of the Jagiellonian University of Kraków for four years, is currently completing his MA studies at the Catholic University of Lublin. His linguistic interests encompass approaches to phonology, the distribution of vocalic length, lenition processes and English dialectology.

TECHNICAL EDITORS
*Jadwiga Makowiec*
*Marta Janiszewska-Hanusiak*

TYPESETTER
*Katarzyna Mróz*

Wydawnictwo Uniwersytetu Jagiellońskiego
Redakcja: ul. Michałowskiego 9/2, 31-126 Kraków
tel. 12-631-18-81, 12-631-18-82, fax 12-631-18-83